Inventive
Fiber Crafts

Elyse Sommer is a crafts designer-author, lecturer, and consultant. Her other books are: *Decoupage Old and New, Rock and Stone Craft, Contemporary Costume Jewelry, Creating with Driftwood and Weathered Wood, A New Look at Crochet, A New Look at Felt, Wearable Crafts, The Bread Dough Craft Book, Make It with Burlap, Designing with Cutouts, Sew Your Own Accessories* (with Joellen Sommer), and *A Patchwork Appliqué and Quilting Primer.*

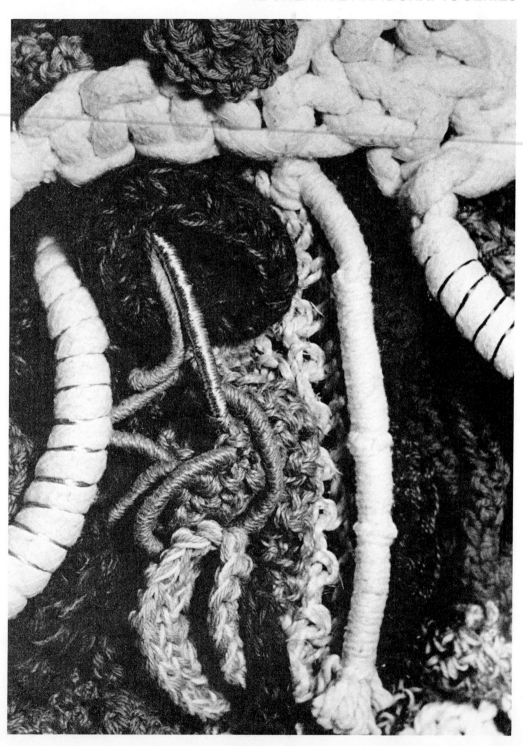

Inventive Fiber Crafts

ELYSE SOMMER

Mike Sommer, *Photographer*

A SPECTRUM BOOK

PRENTICE-HALL, INC., ENGLEWOOD CLIFFS, NEW JERSEY

Library of Congress Cataloging in Publication Data

SOMMER, ELYSE.
   Inventive fiber crafts.

   (A Spectrum Book: The Creative handcrafts
series)
   Bibliography: p.
   1. Textile crafts. I. Sommer, Mike. II. Title.
TT699.S63 1977   746   76-45979
ISBN 0-13-502468-4
ISBN 0-13-502450-1 pbk.

Cover photographs

LEFT — Knotless netted necklace (Maggie Brosnan)

RIGHT (TOP) — *Indian Tassels.* Silk wrapping over linen (Diane Itter)

RIGHT (BOTTOM) — *Lost in the Forest.* Dimensional crochet hanging. Mixed fibers, stones, stuffing. 30″ by 50″ (Elyse Sommer)

Frontispiece

Detail of crocheted, knotted, and wrapped fiber sculpture (Robert Kirchmyer) Photograph by Douglas R. Long

A SPECTRUM BOOK

10 9 8 7 6 5 4 3 2 1

Printed in the United States of America

Prentice-Hall International, Inc. (*London*)
Prentice-Hall of Australia Pty., Ltd. (*Sydney*)
Prentice-Hall of Canada, Ltd. (*Toronto*)
Prentice-Hall of India Private, Limited (*New Delhi*)
Prentice-Hall of Japan, Inc. (*Tokyo*)
Prentice-Hall of Southeast Asia Pte. Ltd. (*Singapore*)
Whitehall Books Limited (*Wellington, New Zealand*)

For the memory of my grandmother,
and the future of her great-granddaughter

Contents

ix

Preface

My grandmother was the first fiber artist I ever knew. She was an expert at knitting, crochet, needlepoint, and tatting. Had someone exposed her to weaving, macramé, wrapping, or coiling, I'm sure she would have become adept at those crafts. I refer to her as an artist though the things she produced were in the handcrafts category. She used her inventiveness within the confines of available knowledge and materials, improvising her own stitches and patterns as she went along and choosing her own color and yarn combinations. My grandmother was also the first fiber artist I knew who earned money with her craft. When she came to the United States, a refugee from Hitler's Germany, a family friend who owned an art and antique gallery immediately bought some of her needlepoint bags and continued to buy whatever she produced. If grandmother were alive today, she would be in the forefront of those who have managed to bridge the gap between handcraft and art in fibers.

Knitting, crochet, and needlework of all kinds continue to give pleasure and relaxation to hobbyists everywhere. The enormous variety of available yarns has expanded the scope of possibilities for even the most inexperienced; magazine articles, books, demonstrations, and classes have built enormous interest in other time-honored skills such as weaving, basketry, knotting, and netting.

One of the major sources of stimulation for making fiber crafts not just a pastime but a legitimate branch of the art scene, to be studied, appreciated, and proudly owned, has been the fantastic innovation by art students and professionals throughout the world. Gallery directors and others in charge of buying art for public spaces have more and more come to recognize the validity of fiber art—its sensuousness, its richness of texture, and its ability to stand the test of time from the point of view of taste and durability.

The fiber crafts which are part of the contemporary art scene are in the tradition of the great tapestries. This twentieth-century renaissance in fibers, owes much to the experimentation with off-loom and non-loom methods, notably those usually classified as hobby or handcrafts. The new shapes and three-dimensional effects being created have given rise to the term *Fiber Sculpture.*

The word "inventive" as applied to fiber crafts does not refer to inventions of tools or methods; instead, inventiveness lies in the ingenuity and vision to adapt the simple and traditional methods to make new statements. To paraphrase a familiar Gilbert and Sullivan quote:

> Old needlework samplers need not be what they seem,
> They can evoke visions of sculpture to those who can dream.

The purpose of this book is to jolt those who think of crafts like knitting and crochet as "just" handcrafts out of their pre-conceived notions. It is hoped that those not already persuaded will recognize the exciting programs possible with the most minimal investments in money and in space. By showing several major fiber commissions in progress, it is hoped that aspiring professionals will gain a clearer picture of studio operations.

Examples of professional work are not limited to large pieces. The biggest is not automatically the best, and it is hoped that the miniature tapestries and sculptures shown will clarify the challenges inherent in solving the problems of both large and small designs.

Instruction for techniques is confined to the rudiments, enough to get the reader started. For in-depth study there are many books devoted entirely to each method covered, and more classes are available each year at all educational levels, including adult education programs and community centers. The techniques chosen for basic instructional demonstrations are by no means the sum total of what might be explored. Tatting, braiding, sprang and cardweaving are some other methods worth the reader's investigation. Every craft presented can be enjoyed on two levels: (1) to make attractive projects for one's pleasure and relaxation (2) to create serious art, small or large.

And so, get out your hook, your needle or tie a warp to a frame or to a tree branch, and put your own inventiveness to work.

Elyse Sommer

Woodmere, Long Island, New York

Acknowledgments

This book is but another step in the rich history of the textile arts. Without the cavemen who had the wit to use their fingers as tools or all those who refined the fabric-making process by improvising needles, hooks, and looms, there would be no traditions to re-explore, there would be no ancient methods to re-learn and re-define.

Without the many contemporary craftspeople who shared their ideas and methods, there would be no *Inventive Fiber Crafts*. A simple thank you hardly suffices. Extraordinary thanks go to Gayle Wimmer, Leora Stewart, and Libby Platus, who have given readers an opportunity to get a clearer understanding of group classroom projects and the development of large fiber commissions. A special note of thanks to all who have encouraged the continued growth of fiber art by initiating educational programs and by using fiber art in their homes and in public places. This is the kind of support and enthusiasm which nourishes the creative spirit.

Inventive
Fiber Crafts

1 Getting Acquainted With Fibers

At the beginning, when you're learning the basics of a particular technique, it doesn't really matter what kinds of yarns you use. Odds and ends collected from friends, bought at sales, or even household string and twine, will do. Pretty soon though, it will become evident that the type of fiber you use is very much a part of the creative process. The yarns which are just right for a garment may be totally wrong for a large wall hanging. The ability to select different materials which will work together in one piece contributes greatly to the successful realization of a concept.

The choice of yarns available today is incredibly rich. Synthetics or man-made fibers, vegetable or plant-derived fibers, animal fibers, plus mixtures of some or all of these can be bought in a broad pallette. Nevertheless, many artists still find that they like to spin and dye their own. Some purchase the yarn already spun, but do their own dyeing. A few have gone back to the ancient process of felting, converting the raw fleece not into yarn but directly into an art fabric.

Whether you plan to get involved in the preliminary fiber processes or not, you will be better able to select and work with materials if you have some understanding of what's involved in spinning, dyeing and felting.

Fig. 1.1 Twin Corriedale lambs grazing at Oldebrooke Spinnery.

HAND SPINNING

To most of us, fleece from which yarn is spun brings instant visions of peaceful sheep roaming and resting in green meadows.

Wool is indeed one of the ideal materials for yarn since it comes in many twists and textures, takes well to dyes and spins into a warm yarn with the elasticity desirable to many fiber crafts. Fleece may, however, be obtained from other kinds of animal hair. A sheep's fleece is usually shorn in one big piece, which is in turn sorted, since some portions of the fleece are of different qualities than others. Some native weavers know just what to pick from which sheep for certain desired results. There is a direct cause and effect relationship between environment and diet and the overall quality of the fleece.

After shearing and sorting, burrs and twigs and other sticky materials must be removed. The fleece must also be thoroughly scoured or washed. It can be dyed at this stage, a process known as dyeing "in the fleece" or after spinning in which case it is spun "in the grease", before the natural lanolin of the sheep is removed. Fleece can be purchased at any of these stages: "In the grease", meaning that you do the picking, scouring, carding, spinning and dyeing; cleaned and dyed; cleaned but undyed (see Sources of Supplies).

In the following photo series Susan Goldin demonstrates carding and spinning undyed wool fleece, using various hand spindles. Dog brushes can be used instead of carders and drop spindles can be improvised from wooden dowels and door knobs, yo-yos or balls made from non-hardening clay.

2

Fig. 1.2 To break down the long hair of raw fleece for spinning, small sections must be pulled apart or teased and then carded as shown here. By carding each clump of fleece several times, the fibers are straightened for good spinning.

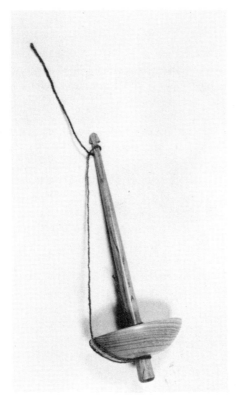

Fig. 1.3 A drop spindle weighing two to three ounces is ideal for beginners. A length of yarn (approximately three feet), known as the leader, is fastened to the spindle. Start by wrapping the yarn several times around the shaft, just above the whorl, Next bring the yarn down over the whorl and secure it around the knob protruding on the bottom of the spindle. Bring the leader back up over the whorl and secure it at the notch near the top with a half hitch.

Fig. 1.4   To start spinning, place a small clump of fleece into the palm of your hand and lay the top end of the leader over the fleece, holding it all down between thumb and forefingers. Now, twist the spindle by touching the top of the shaft . . . then twist the yarn.

Fig. 1.5   Continue the spinning process, using the right hand to keep twisting the spindle clockwise and the left to draw the fibers out in a V position. The fingers should be on the yarn. Never hold the spindle as if it were a teacup, and if it drops, well, that's why it's called a *drop* spindle. Add new clumps of fleece as the original teased fibers are used up or spun.

Fig. 1.6 Here Susan demonstrates spinning with a long Navajo spindle. The shaft is rolled at an angle across the leg. This type of spindle is more difficult to control and is recommended for lower twist yarns.

Fig. 1.7 For very light, fine yarns, Susan uses a Turkish spindle. It has neither knob nor cross bar and spins very fast.

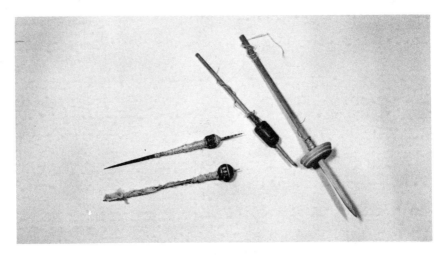

Fig. 1.8 Three small spindles primarily used for spinning fine yarns such as silk. The two spindles at the left have clay balls; the middle spindle is made with a wooden bead whorl.

FELTMAKING

First-time spinners who opt to wash and prepare their own fleece often make the mistake of subjecting the wool to harsh temperature changes during washing. This tends to make the fibers cling together, creating results that are more like cloth than yarn. In fact, the very thing to avoid when washing fleece for spinning is the basis of the ancient process of feltmaking. While most modern feltmaking has become a high-speed production process, the more ancient methods of felting have stirred considerable curiosity among textile students. In primitive felt making (still practiced in portions of Central Asia) the fleece is layered onto a large mat, rubbed with a binding mixture of grease or oil and water. Feltmakers then roll, unroll and reroll the mat for hours. The fabric is exposed to alternate dampening, drying and, finally, stretching. Many early civilizations used these felted fabrics for personal and household adornments. It was a strong and very portable fabric which made it ideal for the tents or yurts used by the early Central Asian nomads.

Modern day experimenters with feltmaking have worked out a variety of adaptations. One of the simplest ways to introduce youngsters to felting is to insert clumps of raw fleece into shoes, to be worn daily for several weeks. For larger pieces of fabric, the household washing machine and dryer can be effectively utilized.

Fig. 1.9 Teased and carded fleece is layered onto a piece of muslin or nylon netting. Colored fleece can be used to create abstract or realistic designs. The thicker the layer of fleece, the thicker the final fabric.

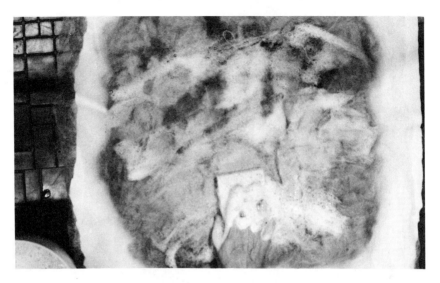

Fig. 1.10 A second piece of muslin or nylon is placed on top of the fleece (very sheer nylon was used here so that the reader can clearly see the process). A sponge is dipped into a bowl of water into which a few drops of detergent have been mixed. By firmly hand sponging the layered felt "sandwich" at this point, the fabric is subjected to a strong, direct binding of the fibers. While this is an optional step, I recommend it to avoid undue shrinkage and to insure a strong fabric.

Fig. 1.11 Fold the felt into a secure package. Pin, then baste through all the layers.

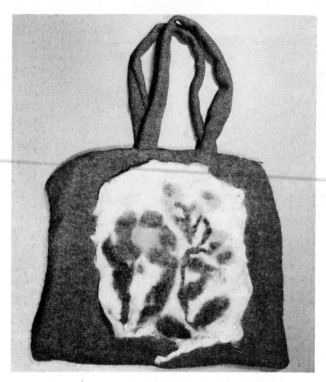

Fig. 1.12 After the felt package is washed in the machine, then dried in a hot drier, it is pressed with a hot steam iron and can be used as desired . . . for example, as an appliqué for a hand-sewn flannel bag by Joellen Sommer.

SHAPED FELTING

Jan Alderson creates lovely, subtly colored shaped fabric forms by molding her fleece over plastic bottles.

Fig. 1.13 Plastic bottles and bowls are a part of Jan's equipment for shaped felting.

Fig. 1.14 Different colors of fleece are teased together into a very thick and fluffy shape.

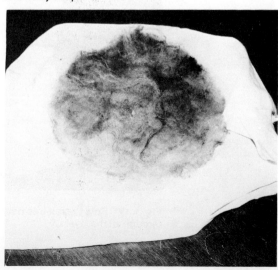

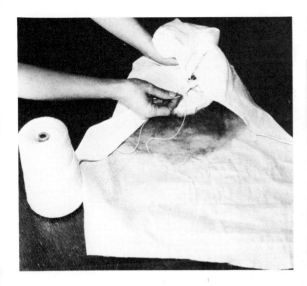

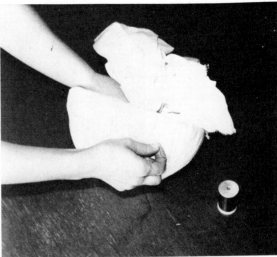

Fig. 1.15 The bottom layer of muslin is drawn up around the container, and the fleece and wrapped very securely with string.

Fig. 1.16 Both layers of muslin and the fleece are quilt stitched to hold the fleece in place. Large stitches are okay.

Fig. 1.17 Jan omits automatic washing, instead scrubbing her fleece with very hot water and lots of soap. A firm circular motion is recommended to entangle the fibers. The felt is dried in the dryer as in the previous demonstration.

Fig. 1.18 To create her flowerlike shapes, the artist often finds additional shrinkage desirable and to effect this she wraps a ball of polyester fiberfill in muslin, places it in the felted shape. She then rewraps the whole shape, wets it thoroughly once again and returns it to the dryer.

9

Fig. 1.19 Shaped felt pieces are stitched to a handmade felt backing.

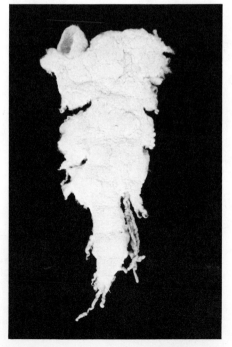

Fig. 1.20 Sometimes the artist uses fine quilt stitching for her flat pieces of felt and then leaves the muslin in place for rear-view interest.

The process of making paper is similar to feltmaking. Natural plant materials are "felted" in boiled water and lye. Debra Rapoport has at times combines both felt and paper. A large three-part wall hanging designed for the Nik-Nik showrooms in New York can be seen in the color section.

Fig. 1.21 Mary Anderson creates small woven baskets from handmade paper.

YARN DYEING

In addition to dyeing one's own yarn with natural plant materials, one can also choose from many excellent dyes on the market. Instructions for mordants, duration of immersion, are available in books and many inexpensive booklets (see bibliography) or on the dye packages. To dye a skein of yarn, tie it in several places with string to prevent tangling and dip into a large pot into which dye and hot water have been mixed.

A very simple and fun way of experimenting with dyeing is to space dye the yarn in a random pattern. For example, wind a ball of wool, keeping your finger in the center as you wind it. Place powdered dye onto the tip of a spoon and insert into the hole at the center of the ball.

Fig. 1.22 A novel way of space dyeing calls for winding a ball of yarn so that a hole is formed at the center. Powdered dye is spooned into this hole and then sealed in by continuing to wind the ball.

Continue to wind the ball, covering the hole and thus locking in the dye powder. Immerse the ball into hot water and swish it around. The variegated yarn can be allowed to dry on the ball. This method is primarily for creating an ombre type of yarn with one color. White yarn, for example, will have different shades of brown and tan if brown dye is used.

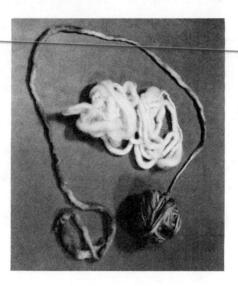

Fig. 1.23 White yarn space dyed in shades of brown.

If you want to use more than one color, lay a skein of yarn on to a piece of tinfoil in a shallow baking pan. Sprinkle on different colors at random. Pour just a little water over the yarn and bake in the oven to set the colors.

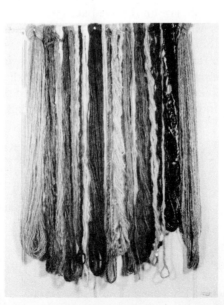

Fig. 1.24 Hand-spun and hand-dyed yarns, like this lovely assortment by Susan Goldin, add colorful and decorative accents wherever they're hung, without any further manipulation.

Weaving on Looms of Many Shapes
2 and Materials

The process of weaving horizontal threads known as wefts, through vertical threads or warps is as old as the story of mankind. At the very beginning, men twined weft threads over and under stiffened reeds or rushes laid out on the ground. To make the process easier and more comfortable, the primitive weaver drove two sticks into the ground in between which a horizontal cross bar was attached. To this cross bar the warp threads were tied. To make the warp rigid and thus facilitate the task of passing the weft back and forth, stones or other weights were tied to the bottom of the warp threads.

Eventually those who weave a lot will want to invest in and learn to use a modern loom with its time-saving features. However, weaving by hand remains a primary method even for professional studio weavers because of the flexibility of the warping and weaving methods, and the greater intimacy with materials and designs many feel when working in this way.

*Weaving
on Looms
of Many Shapes
and Materials*

Fig. 2.1 Twined ruglet from Ethiopia, from the collection of Nancy Bess.

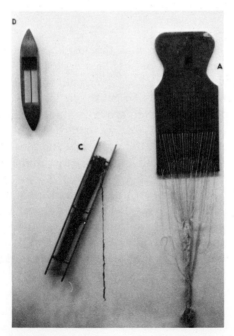

Fig. 2.2 Early weaving tools from the collection of the Museum at Stony Brook, New York. The tape loom (A), once popular for band weaving, is somewhat similar to stick weaving described later in this chapter.

The illustrations in the following pages give ample proof that the simplicity of the loom in no way restricts the inventive weaver from creating designs ranging from small finger rings (Chapter 3, Fig. 3-13) to wall-sized hangings.

BASIC WEAVES ON A NOTCHED CARBOARD LOOM

Any firm cardboard can be converted into a handy and portable loom. Notches or slits are evenly spaced at each end of the board. Warping proceeds from a continuous ball of yarn. The warp can be brought all around from front to back; the warp can also be kept at the front of the loom by warping only around the points of the notches. The latter method enables you to slip the completed weaving off the loom with the edges all finished. Notched looms can be round, irregular or shaped like a garment.

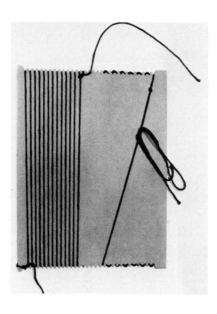

Fig. 2.3 Rear view of notched cardboard loom, showing one side warped from front to back and one side with only the front of the loom warped.

To weave, you need tapestry or weaving needles with eyes large enough to hold the weft yarn (many weavers wind up long lengths of yarn into bundles or butterflies and use their fingers to weave), scissors to cut yarn and a comb for pushing or "beating" the weft close together. To raise the warp from the cardboard, several thicknesses of cardboard can be taped to either side of the loom. As the weaving progresses and tightens, these sticks can be removed. A taped cardboard stick or ruler can be used to create a shed which makes it possible to pass the weaving weft through the warps in one motion every other row. When this shed stick is flattened, the warp threads to be woven are picked up individually.

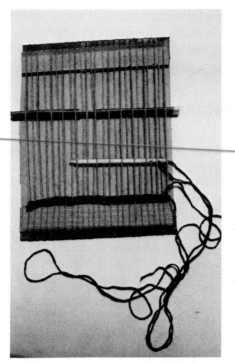

Fig. 2.4 A notched cardboard loom with extra thickness of cardboard taped to each end of the loom in order to raise the warp up. A piece of cardboard is folded and taped to serve as a shed stick. When the stick is raised on its side, as seen here, the weft can be passed through all the warps to be woven in one motion. For the following row, the shed will be flattened and the warps picked out one by one.

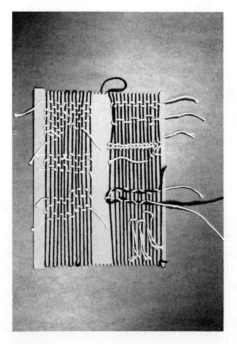

Fig. 2.5 Here we see the front of Fig. 2.3, with the most popular weaves illustrated at the right side and patterns of weaving at the left. *Right, top to bottom:* (1) Tabby weave—the weft goves over one warp, under the next. (2) Basket weave—the weft is passed over two and under two. (3) Wrapped or soumak weave—each warp thread is enclosed. (4) Twined weaving—two wefts are worked simultaneously, one going over and the other under the same warp. (5) Rya knots— pre-cut lengths are passed over and between two warps, creating a raised pile surface. Rows of plain weaving are usually alternated with the knots to hold them in place. *Left, top to bottom:* (1) Two wefts can be woven separately within one row to create color patterns. When the wefts meet without joining, a slit is created. (2) The separate wefts can also be interlocked, a process known as dovetailing. (3) There are all sorts of variations in slit weave patterns.

Fig. 2.6 Necklace woven on a shaped cardboard loom, using tabby weave, with beads and feathers strung and tied to the loose ends. Melany Lynch.

Fig. 2.7 Shaped cardboard woven necklace, with soumak or wrapped weaving. Melany Lynch.

Fig. 2.8 Madge Copeland constructed an irregular cardboard loom to conform to the outlines of a piece of plywood. The warp of the weaving was extended to go through holes drilled into the wood. Flattened eucalyptus bark, pieces of leather, fur and driftwood were glued and nailed to the wood. Photo, Keith Brewster.

Fig. 2.9 The warp ends of Madge Copeland's wood weaving were knotted and glued at the rear of the plywood.

WIRES AND HOOPS

Discarded bicycle rims, hoola hoops, steel rings and embroidery hoops may be utilized as looms which can remain a permanent part of the weaving. Hoops can be warped vertically, with horizontal threads acting as both warp and weft; they can be warped in a circular fashion, like the spokes on a wheel, with the weft going all around; or in a simple vertical warp pattern.

Fig. 2.10 Jennifer Smith, a student in Alice Sprintzen's Oyster Bay High School crafts class, used an embroidery hoop as her loom for this beautiful weaving sampler.

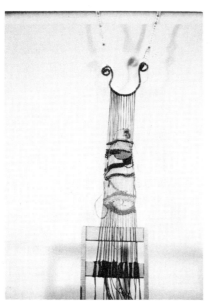

Fig. 2.11 Heavy gauge wire is wrapped, shaped, and attached to an exposed ceiling pipe. The warp threads are mounted with Lark's Head knots (Chapter 6, fig. 6.1) and tied to the top of a chair. The weaving can begin at any point, meander in any direction.

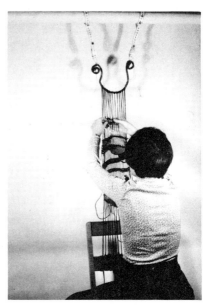

Fig. 2.12 The weaver straddles the chair, and the weaving process has much of the intimacy associated with the primitive backstrap loom, except that the warp ends are attached to the chair instead of around the weaver's waist. Anyone liable to frequent work interruptions will appreciate this difference.

19

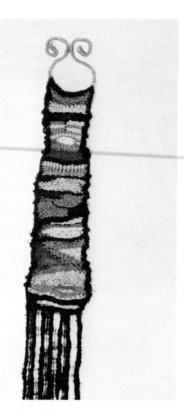

Fig. 2.13 Crocheted mohair is used to finish the sides and fringes.

FRAME LOOMS, LARGE AND SMALL

A frame loom, even when constructed on a floor-to-ceiling size scale, is no more complicated than the devices presented so far. The larger the loom, the stronger the frame pieces should be. Small frames can be notched, like the cardboard variety. The warp can also be wound around nails hammered at angles (see Fig. 2-17).

When using a small decorative frame, wrapping nails can be kept at the back, with the warp brought around the back only. The loom can thus serve as a frame for the finished work.

A double warp can be created by bringing the warp all around the frame. The frame creates a space between front and back warp threads. The weaver can weave each warp separately, weave the two warps as one, or switch from single to double warp methods within a piece and thus create tubes and pockets. On a large frame the double warp is effected by placing nails on both sides of the frame and warping both sides. This will be seen in the demonstration which follows.

Fig. 2.14 This weaving represents a joint effort by students in Gayle Wimmer's Off-Loom Weaving Class at Hunter College. Robin Koenig, Shelley Krepes, Marilyn Sibrizzi, Paul Sheridan, and Susan Tam constructed the loom and worked as a group, with Robin Koenig keeping a photographic record of the work as it progressed.

Fig. 2.15 The space between front and back warps enabled students to work on both sides simultaneously.

Fig. 2.16 When front and back warps were to be woven together as one, group conferences with the instructor helped in making decisions about color changes and shapes.

Fig. 2.17 The finished weaving is cut from the nails, two warps at a time. The rags tied to the sides of the weaving were put in temporarily to keep the weaving from pulling.

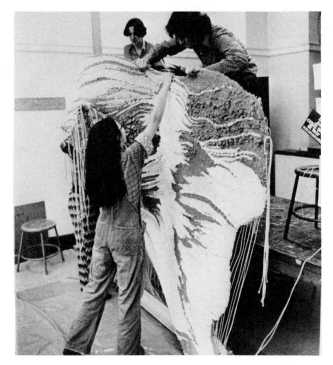

Fig. 2.18 This is an exciting and tense period, with all hands needed.

Fig. 2.19 Plastic sheeting was spread out to protect the work as it came off the loom. It can also serve as a protective casing for rolling up the work and transporting it to its final destination.

24.

*Weaving
on Looms
of Many Shapes
and Materials*

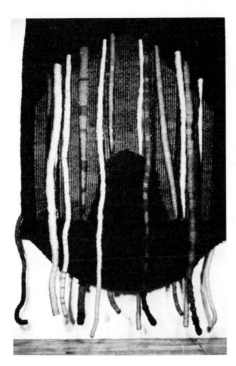

Fig. 2.20 Gayle Wimmer installed the same type of frame loom as the one just seen in her studio. This dramatic hanging of grey and black wools on heavy jute warp is particularly notable for the long, flexible tubes. The tubes are woven, not wrapped. To weave the tubes, Gayle had to start her weaving from the top, standing on a ladder and literally working upside down. The top part of the weaving utilized the two warps as one. The tubes were made by weaving *around and around*, not back and forth, sections of the front warp.

Fig. 2.21 This very tactile and dimensional type of hanging invites play and participation. Here the artist "plays" with just some of the variations possible.

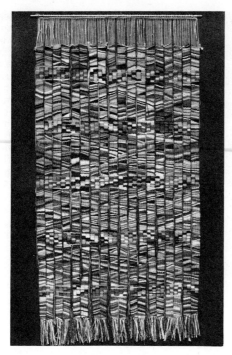

Fig. 2.22 Diane Itter's *Peru* illustrates more vividly than any words the creative possibilities of frame loom weaving on a very small scale. The artist likes to experiment with color interaction and uses very fine materials. Her warp is linen and her weft a mixture of cotton, linen, rayon, wool, and silk. The entire piece measures just 11 inches by 20 inches (see color section).

Fig. 2.23 *Peru* was worked in sections . . .

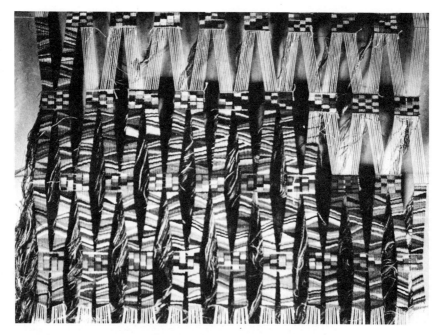

Fig. 2.24 Connected at random.

Fig. 2.25 The back of the weaving does not reveal the pattern, since the artist decided to leave the many weft ends loose to create a shaglike surface.

FROM SMALL FRAME TO NO FRAME

Eileen Senner has used her inventiveness to overcome the problems of the artist who wants to create large pieces but whose circumstances limit her to a small working space. She uses heavy jute for her warp and begins her weaving by tying the jute to one end of a smallish frame, using any old knot that will hold. She makes the opposite warp end into a butterfly and attaches that to the opposite end of the frame, using a slip knot. Next, she weaves within the frame just long enough to get her weaving started and after that she depends upon her feet and hands to give her the tension to continue her weaving without any loom at all, until it measures some twelve feet in length. The in-progress photos of Eileen's work were taken by John W. Senner; the photos of her finished work are by Stephen Anderson.

Fig. 2.26 Heavy jute warp is square knotted to one end of a frame, tied into a butterfly and slip knotted to the other end. Fourteen warp threads will be used to create a five-inch wide band.

Fig. 2.27   The weaving proceeds inside the frame for about 8 inches, long enough to create sufficient tension.

Fig. 2.28   Once the warp is untied from the frame foot, pressure is applied to one part, while the hands are used to separate the warp and continue the weaving.

Fig. 2.29   The weaving progresses, maintaining the foot
pressure and using the hands to beat the weft.

Fig. 2.30   The band builds up
around the weaver. As the end of the
warp comes into view, additional
warps can be added . . .

Fig. 2.31 slit woven and reattached to the end of the band, with or without the interest-adding knot.

Fig. 2.32 The finished fiber piece.

For super portablity and simplicity consider the humble dowel. By drilling holes at one end of the dowel and sanding the other end to a point, warp threads can be strung onto the dowels and the weaving worked around the sticks which serve as the rigid part of the warp. As the sticks are filled with the weaving, the weft is pushed off the stick and onto the warp threads.

Dowels ranging in thickness from 1/2" to 3/4" can be used. Thicker dowels permit you to drill larger holes which in turn accomodate thicker warp yarns. Each dowel should be cut into 6- to 9-inch lengths, depending upon the thickness used. Sand the holed ends just enough to round off the sharp edges which will make the weft slip off more smoothly.

To warp the stick loom, cut warp twice as long as you want the finished piece to be, plus an allowance for fringes. You can use one very thick warp thread doubled over, or several strands doubled. The weft is woven off a continuous ball or skein of wool. You can weave in an under or over or tabby pattern; you can wrap each stick, soumak fashion, which tends to create a natural tube. You can even twine two wefts.

Weave in a fairly loose manner so the weaving pushes down onto the warp threads easily. Be sure to leave some weaving on the sticks at all times. New colors can be tied in at random. Different colors can be stranded together for tweed effects. Variegated or space-dyed yarns are very effective. When the bands are the desired length, the warps are cut off the sticks. Warps can be pulled and twisted, causing the weaving to curve and bend. Thus, with a method easy enough for very young children to learn, sophisticated design experiments are possible.

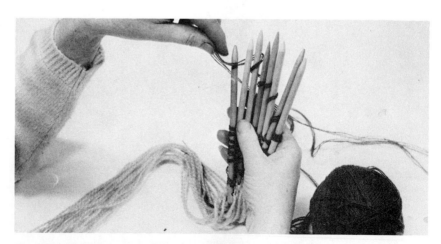

Fig. 2.33 Wrapped or soumak weaving around an eight-stick loom. As few as two and as many as ten sticks can be used. Different yarns can be stranded together for a single weft.

Fig. 2.34 Stick-weaving samples. From right to left: Tabby, soumak, and twining with a random pattern of color changes; an all-soumak sample; raffia weft and warp might be used to make strong plant holders.

Fig. 2.35 When a soumak woven weft is very tightly beaten, a natural tube forms. The warp can also be pulled to create extraordinary tension, as seen at right.

**Weaving
on Looms
of Many Shapes
and Materials**

Fig. 2.36 A soumak woven band has been twisted to curve around a mirror, encasing it quite firmly. The warp ends are wrapped together for a decorative tassel. The puffy yarn knob is an idea borrowed from Madge Copeland. Yarn is wrapped loosely around the core in a horizontal direction. When this horizontal wrapping is nice and full, a needle is threaded and brought over and under in a vertical pattern. The vertical wrap stitching continues until the horizontal threads are all covered.

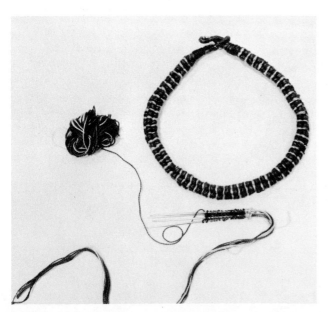

Fig. 2.37 The stick-weaving technique can also be adapted to very fine warps and wefts. In this case, large-eyed embroidery needles are used for the loom, as illustrated in a necklace of variegated cotton—in process and finished.

Fig. 2.38 Needle-woven basket. Four bands of lightweight wool are woven on a loom of six embroidery needles, stitched together to form a basket. The warp ends are wrapped in mohair and stitched down to form the ring edge.

Fig. 2.39 Bottom view of needle-woven basket, showing how bands were intertwined.

Fig. 2.40 Hat made with band of variegated handspun wool twined on a 6-dowel loom.

Fig. 2.41 The top of the hat is made on two warped embroidery needles, with the narrow band stitched into a coil. The crown and brim of the hat are connected wtih crochet.

Fig. 2.42 Mary Lou Higgins always has a ready supply of long stick-woven bands to use as "stage sets" for her crocheted figures.

SHAPING THE WARP ON A PIN WARP LOOM

The pin warp loom affords the weaver the advantage of making the warping pattern conform to the final shape desired. A cellutex or foam board and round headed pins are all that's needed. The warp can be wound around the pins in the same way as on a nailed or notched frame or board loom, the only diference being that the pins are inserted as the warping progresses. Yvonne Porcella has developed a method of attaching separate warps with Lark's Head mountings (Chapter 6, Fig. 6-1) around the top pin; each end cord is individually pinned. Yvonne feels that the fact that this method permits her to repin cords as she is actually weaving more than compensates in versatility for the greater time required for warping. She has created several manquettes to demonstrate the pin loom shaping process.

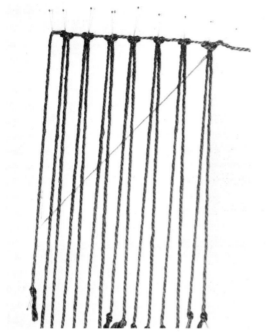

Fig. 2.43 The warp is pinned in place for a beginning triangle shape.

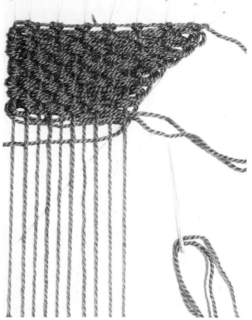

Fig. 2.44 A single warp thread is unpinned and woven along with the weft to form a bias edge.

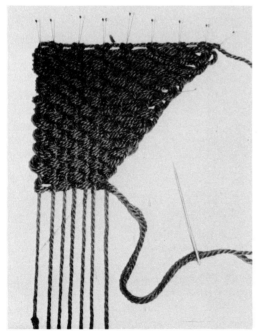

Fig. 2.45 The triangle continues to develop, with warps unpinned and woven with the weft. The triangle will be completed when all the warps have been unpinned and woven.

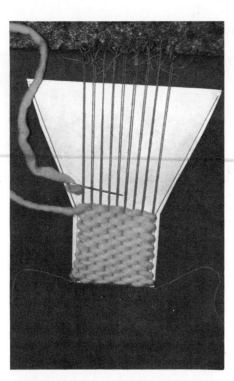

Fig. 2.46 A narrow-to-wide shape is developed by weaving through two warp threads at a time . . .

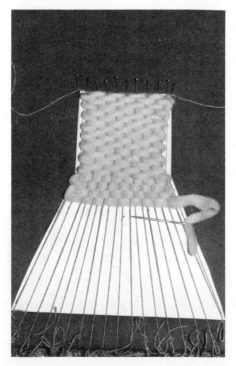

Fig. 2.47 and separating the threads for the wider section.

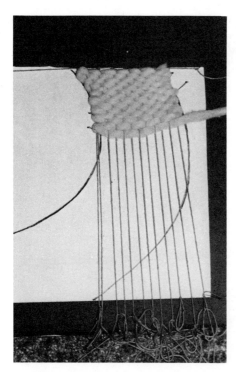

Fig. 2.48 A circular or collar shape is drawn on paper and threads are pinned to the top edge in a fanned-out pattern at the distant point.

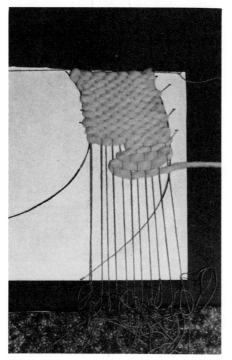

Fig. 2.49 Warps are unpinned and woven with the weft to follow the shape.

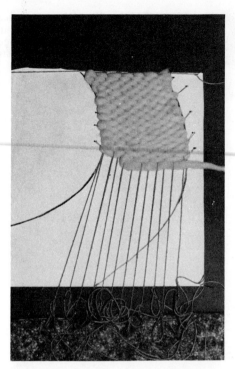

Fig. 2.50 The outside edge is increased with extra weft to even up the design.

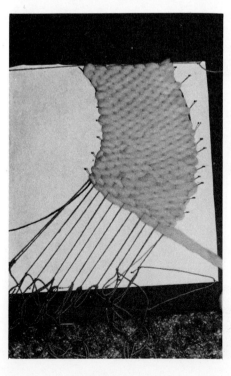

Fig. 2.51 The weaving progresses in conformity with the pattern.

WEAVING A VEST ON A PIN WARP LOOM

Yvonne Porcella now shows how her method of pin loom weaving would work in the creation of a garment.

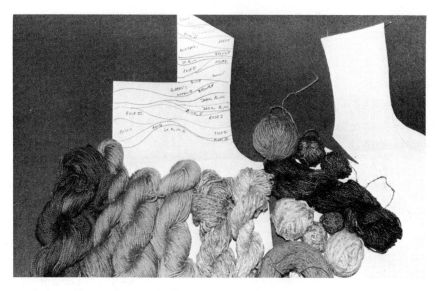

Fig. 2.52 Using a commercial vest pattern as a guide, Yvonne plans her design on paper. Linen will be used for the warp, since it's shiny and smooth and allows for smooth packing of the weft. Hand-dyed wools and rayons will be used to create the design.

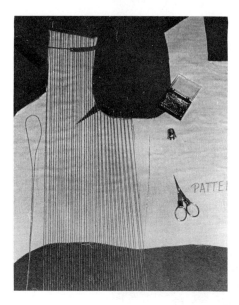

Fig. 2.53 A scrap fabric pattern was tried on for fit (the garment cannot be checked for fit as the weaving progresses) and then pinned to the pattern board. Here we see the beginning of the pin-warp process. The Lark's Head knots at the top are 3/8" apart, the cords at the far end are spaced 1/4" apart.

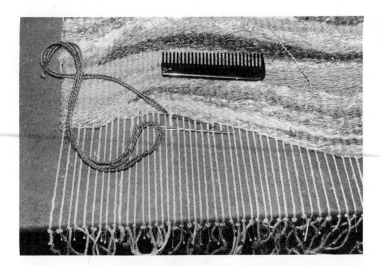

Fig. 2.54 The weaving pattern develops.

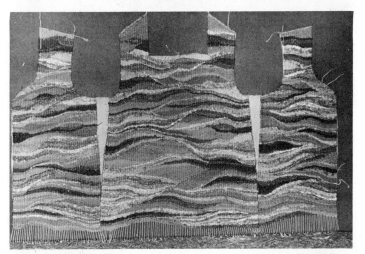

Fig. 2.55 The finished garment is in three sections. The original plan was to weave it all in one piece, however, when the artist decided to lengthen to lower edge, she had to readjust the warp threads and do her weaving in sections. Without the separate pinning of the far warps, this kind of impromptu change would not be possible.

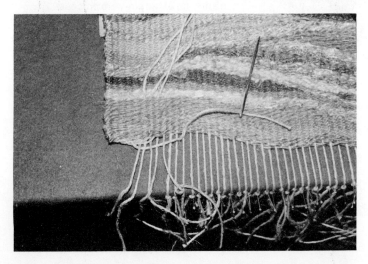

Fig. 2.56 Before the weaving is removed from the board, Yvonne fingerweaves the lower edge by unpinning six warp threads, cutting or untying the knot and weaving the first thread over and under to the sixth space. The warp thread is then threaded onto the needle and up into the weaving. This continues until all the warp threads are woven.

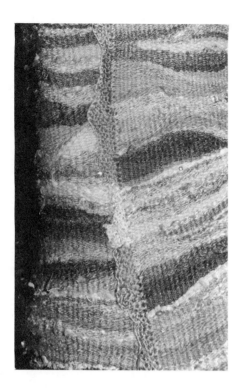

Fig. 2.57 Side seams are made with knotless netting rather than sewing (see Chapter 7).

Fig. 2.58 Suzanne Porcella models the finished vest.

3 Wrapping and Coiling

Wrapping is used so often with weaving and macramé to add contrast and to create finished ends that many people think of it as a weaving or macramé technique. Yet, wrapping all by itself has proved so versatile and effective that it is indeed a popular craft in its own right. As a teaching method, it is an ideal introduction to the interaction of assorted fibers. It is one of those instantly learned methods, easily visualized, enabling even those who normally have difficulty working spontaneously to do so.

The core or warp around which wrapping is done can be thick rope, bundles of old yarn, anything. Wire inserted into the core facilitates the wrapping and makes the form more flexible and sturdy. The applications of wrapping are scattered throughout this book and this chapter can only begin to picture some of the possibilities of wrapping as an independent craft.

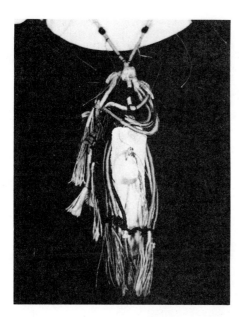

Fig. 3.1 Necklace of silk-wrapped linen with shells, stones, and feathers. Jean Boardman Knorr.

Fig. 3.2 Experimentation with a variety of wools and synthetics grew into a five-foot-tall hanging by Nancy Carter. Photo, Doug Long.

Fig. 3.3 Another wrapped sculpture by Nancy Carter, photographed by Doug Long at the Cathedral of St. John the Divine during a Contemporary Fiber Show.

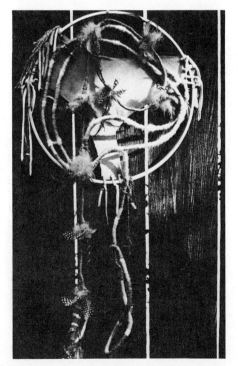

Fig. 3.4 *Reservations* is part of a series by Lily Lowhead, incorporating bells, feathers, suede, and wrapping. This piece began with the suede and the hoop, with cords wrapped and then shaped and attached through holes drilled into different areas of the hoop.

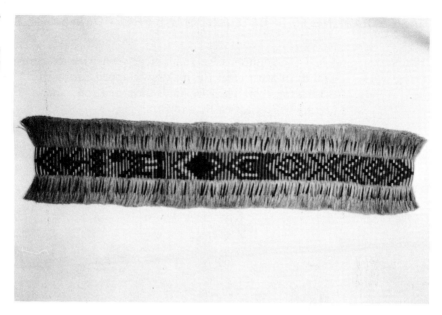

Fig. 3.5 Wrapping can be planned to conform to a precisely graphed pattern, like cross-stitch embroidery. Each piece of this handsome little mat was individually wrapped (see color section). Diane Itter.

Fig. 3.6 Here is a section of the color graph and one of the wrapped sections for *Tassels*. Note the two loose threads which have been wrapped in with the bundled linen warp. These were used to connect the individually wrapped sections at the rear of the mat, using macramé knots. (see Chapter 6).

BASIC WRAPPING TO CREATE RINGS AND FREE FORM SHAPES

I find the addition of aluminum or steel wire to a warp of eight or ten strands of yarn ideal for making wrapped forms which will be bent and twisted together. The wire holds the core firmly and is also useful for connecting warp ends easily and firmly.

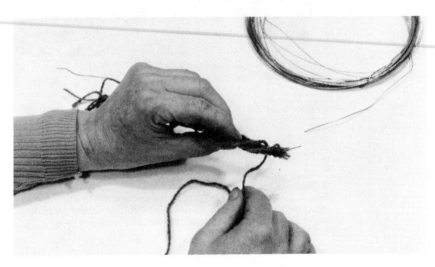

Fig. 3.7 A length of bundled yarn and wire which will be shaped into a ring is started at the end, wrapping from the edge to the left.

Fig. 3.8 The wrapping continues. As weft yarn runs out, lay in a new thread over the old one and continue on. Never work with wefts that are more than a yarn or so in length.

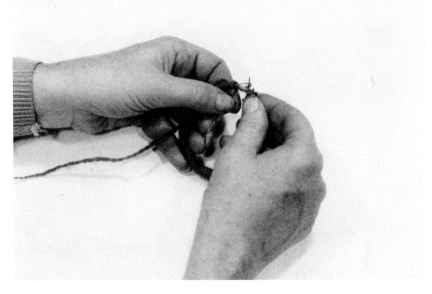

Fig. 3.9 To form and close the ring, make a loop at one side of the wire, and bring the other end of the wire through that loop, as shown.

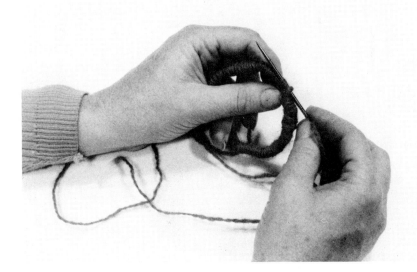

Fig. 3.10 After the second wire has been twisted into a loop, the weft is tightly wrapped around the connected ends and finished by passing the threaded needle through a number of the wraps. The long ends of the weft can be left hanging and used to connect the rings to one another.

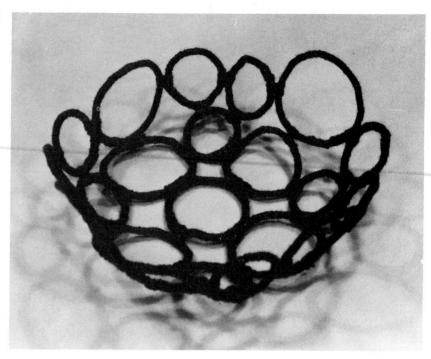

Fig. 3.11 Two sizes of rings have been joined into a simple basket form.

Fig. 3.12 The circle could also be twisted into a rectangular shape and warped for weaving. When the weaving is complete . . .

Fig. 3.13 the frame can be bent to encircle a finger. Without a doubt, this is the smallest weaving in these pages.

Fig. 3.14 To make a continuous wire and yarn wrapped free-form shape, use long lengths of warp and a somewhat heavier gauge wire. Whenever you wish to move in a new direction, bring portions of the wrapping together and connect by bringing the weft from the warp being wrapped, under the section to be joined, as shown in the photo, then over and back to the area to be wrapped. For a very strong "join," repeat this step two or three times. Repeat this process whenever you want to shape and connect.

Fig. 3.15 Free-form wrapped shape to function as tabletop or hanging sculpture. Some of the openings have been filled with crochet. Needle weaving would work equally well. Feathers and beads have been wrapped in for added detail.

COILING

When a wrapped core is formed into a continuous spiral the developing shape is bound by passing the wrapping weft under and over two areas of wrapped warp, as shown in Figure 3-14, and again in the following demonstration by Fred Morrison. Fred uses heavy jute for his warp core and wool to wrap it. Coiling is a slow-moving process. When coiling a large basket each round requires more and more wrapping and will take longer to complete. The advantage of using thick fibers soon become self-evident.

Fig. 3.16 Start the core of the coil about two inches from the edge of the warp, wrapping from right to left.

Fig. 3.17 Bend the wrapped beginning back to form a loop and tighten with a slip knot.

Fig. 3.18 Continue wrapping and shaping, attaching the coil by bringing the needle up through the center of the coil below . . .

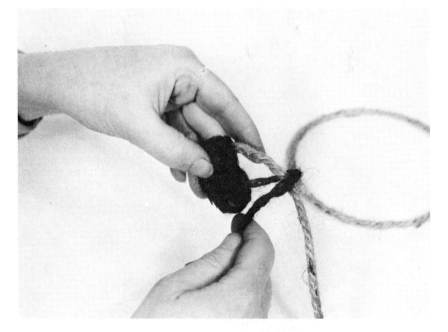

Fig. 3.19 and back around the outside core to continue the wrapping.

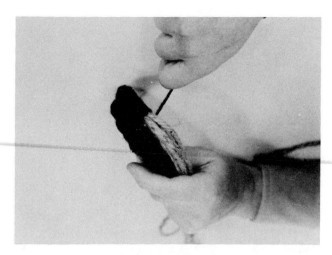

Fig. 3.20 To build up the shape, lay the warp on top of the previous row.

Fig. 3.21 To strengthen the walls of the basket, add additional warp yarn. Add only one cord at a time, so that all the warps are different lengths; this allows you to simply wrap in a new warp cord as you do for added weft.

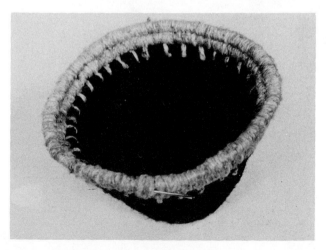

Fig. 3.22 The basket is completed with the weft-threaded needle pushed through several wrapped stitches, ready to be pulled tight and cut off.

Fig. 3.23 A basket coiled exactly like the preceding demonstration model, with silver mylar wrapped over the basic black core. Fred Morrison.

Fig. 3.24 Separate coiled shapes in greys and beiges are appliquéd to a black coiled basket. Pre-cut lengths of white synthetic fibers are needle-netted right through the coils. Black Persian lamb from an old coat was given new life as a lining for this physically and artistically strong piece. Fred Morrison.

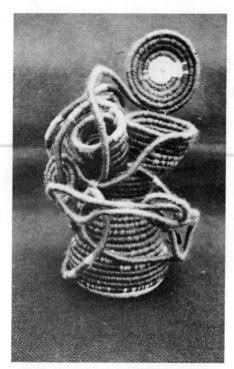

Fig. 3.25 This beautiful basket by Lynn Myers combines coiling and wrapping.

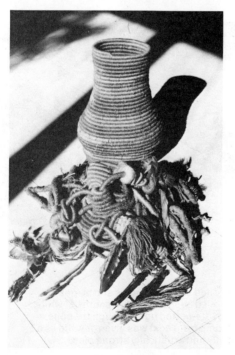

Fig. 3.26 *Pot Head* has an elaborately coiled and feathered lid (see color section). Madge Copeland.

Fig. 3.27 A small, well-shaped coiled container of waxed linen, with coconut button accents. Nancy Bess.

Fig. 3.28 Simple coils with interesting free-form twists lend themselves to decorative and functional designs like this bottle holder and mat by Nancy Bess.

Fig. 3.29 Madge Copeland wrapped and coiled clothesline rope with grey and brown wool. She calls her dimensional hanging *I Am Woman*. Photo, Keith Brewster.

Fig. 3.30 Another coiled and wrapped hanging, this one combining a mixture of yarns with feathers and handmade machie beads. Hanna Lederman.

Fig. 3.31 Coils can be used to encase a variety of hard objects. This sculptural form was made in the free-form wire-wrapped method described earlier in this chapter. The coils holding ink-drawn shells and wooden discs are worked into the joined sections. The method for making the yarn puffs is described in Chapter 2, fig. 2.36.

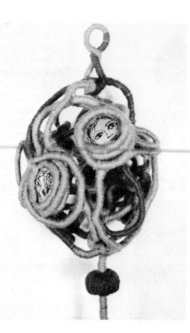

Fig. 3.32 Detail view of wrapped
and coiled sculpture.

TWINING BASKETS AND BASKET SHAPES

Coiled baskets are built with a single element center, joined by means of a
flexible wrapped weft. Twining, another popular and ancient basketry
method, builds the shape from a center of multiple elements which are then
wrapped or twined with a double weft. Twining can be used on a flat woven
surface, as already seen in Chapter 2.

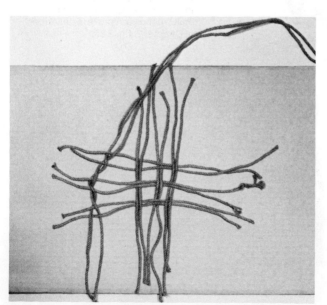

Fig. 3.33 Twined baskets start
with a center of interlaced yarns
around which weft is twined.
Additional elements are added as
the shape grows.

Fig. 3.34 The many loose ends of a twined basket call upon the artist's inventiveness with finishing touches. Here, Nancy Bess has tucked her ends inside her twined basket in a strikingly decorative effect.

Fig. 3.35 Bottom view of the twined basket.

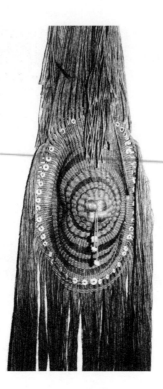

Fig. 3.36 Susan Goldin bundles
and intertwines many warp threads
for a twined center from which she
builds a very dimensional hanging in
soft beige and blue, with button
accents.

Fig. 3.37 Another of Susan
Goldin's basket hangings. This one
combines twining and coiling.

4 Creative Knitting

> The most resourceful and inventive method of fiber construction in the world, being made without loom or machine, without warp or weft, shaped as it is constructed, patterned as whim requires, and divided without being cut!
>
> *Mary Thomas's Knitting Book*[1]

Of all the fiber crafts, knitting has enjoyed the longest and most uninterrupted popularity as an enjoyable, creative and useful skill. Its origins have been traced back to pre-Christian times, to the nomads of the Arabian Desert. In Tudor and Elizabethan England when craft guilds thrived, knitting, like weaving, was done by men who had to serve stringent apprenticeships—three years to learn the basics and another three years to learn the techniques of other countries. According to Mary Thomas, to become a master knitter the apprentice had to complete a carpet measuring six feet by five feet, with a design containing flowers, foliage, birds and animals in natural colors, as well as several garments.

[1](New York: Dover Publications, 1972)

Contemporary fiber artists have done somewhat less experimental knitting than crocheting. Yet, much can be done, and those who have explored knitting as art have not been disappointed. Both Ron King, with his knitted weavings, and Norma Minkowitz, with her pristine sculptures and hangings, have put their own unmistakable stamps upon contemporary knit art. Many knitters have used and adapted that familiar children's toy, the knitting Jenny to create exciting jewelry as well as architectural space forms. Since knitting and crocheting seem to go almost hand in hand, the mixing of the two skills has opened up still other avenues. Stitch patterns are fun to master and people like Mary Walker Phillips and Barbara Walker have published enough books of patterns to keep readers knitting for years. Only basic stitches need be mastered to create knit art as will be seen in the pages which follow.

KNITTING BASICS

In the photo series which follows, you will learn how to cast on stitches, to make the two basic stitches (knit and purl), to cast off, to increase and decrease. Shaping and patterns can be created simply by varying the size of one's ability to increase and decrease. Wooden knitting needles, one stained dark, are used to facilitate the reader's comprehension.

CASTING ON STITCHES

Fig. 4.1 To cast on, place a slip stitch onto the dark needle, insert the light needle as shown, and bring the yarn around the front.

Fig. 4.2 Retract the point of the light needle, but keep the stitch on the dark one as shown. Next, twist the light needle around to the back of the dark needle and . . .

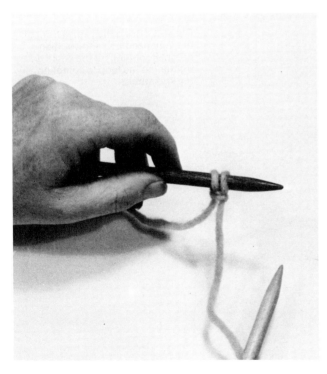

Fig. 4.3 place the loop from the light needle next to the one on the dark, thus completing your first two stitches cast on.

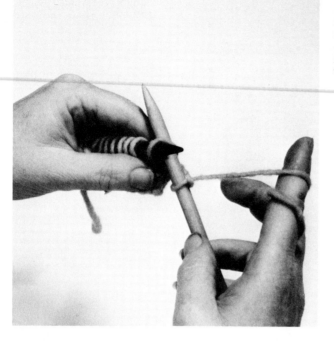

Fig. 4.4 With the desired number of stitches cast onto the dark needle, begin knitting by inserting the light needle into the back of the stitch (variations can be achieved by inserting the needle into the front of the stitch).

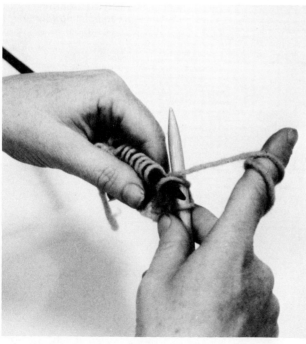

Fig. 4.5 Bring the yarn in front of the light needle as shown, then retract it, pulling off the stitch and tightening the loop to complete the knit stitch.

Creative Knitting

Fig. 4.6 If every row is done in a knit stitch, both sides of the knitting will look like the sample at the top. The smooth pattern of the bottom sample is achieved by making every other row in the pure stitch.

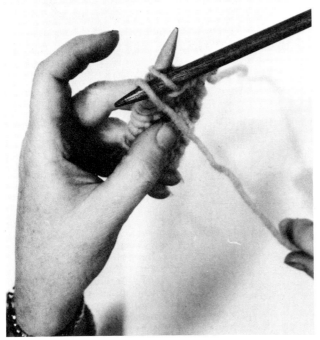

Fig. 4.7 After your first row of knitting, all the stitches will be on the light needle. To purl, insert the dark needle from back to front and bring the yarn around as shown.

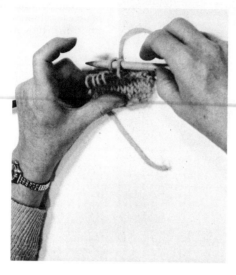

Fig. 4.8 To bind off or finish a piece of knitting, knit two stitches and then pick up the first stitch and pull it over the second as shown. When the next stitch is made, this remaining stitch becomes the first of the two to be pulled over or bound off.

SHAPING

Knitting can be shaped by increasing and decreasing. To increase, knit into the back of the stitch, and make another stitch into the front. Another way of increasing is to knit a stitch, pass the yarn around the needle before knitting the next stitch. This produces a hole when you work back across the row and knit the yarn-overs as if they were regular stitches. More than one yarn-over creates large lacey holes. To decrease, knit two stitches together.

Fig. 4.9 Here are three examples of shaping with increases and shaping with increases and decreases: (1) Top left: The spool shape is made by decreasing one stitch at each edge of the knitting, until a triangle develops; to reverse the triangle and create the spool, increases are made at each end. (2) The lacy square was made by making random increases with yarn-overs. (3) The ruffly shape at the bottom was produced by knitting one row with an increase made into every stitch, purling back, and then decreasing into every stitch. This pattern of expansion and subtraction creates the ruffles or puffs, which can be made more or less pronounced by varying the patterns of increases and decreases.

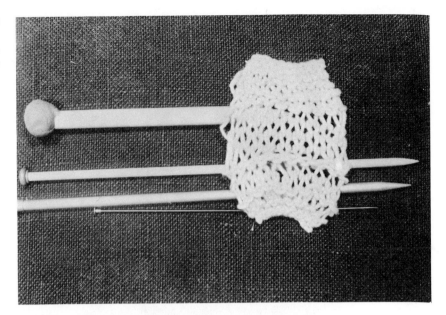

Fig. 4.10 What seems like different stitch patterns is actually
all one stitch, but each row was knitted with different sized
needles. The bottom needle was fashioned from a dowel
pointed with sandpaper. The protective tip is made of
plastilene rolled into a bead and glued around the dowel.

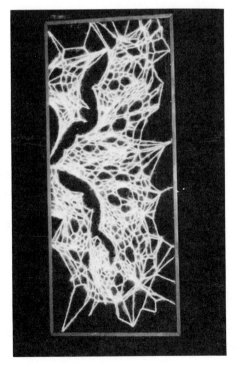

Fig. 4.11 This intriguing bat-
shaped hanging by Nancy Lipe
consists of three separate pieces knit
with random yarn-overs to create the
holes. The stretchy nylon mohair
used permitted the artist to further
manipulate the shapes to conform
to her design image.

**Creative
Knitting**   A necklace is a good starting project for experimenting with unusual materials, creating shapes and holes and tubular bands.

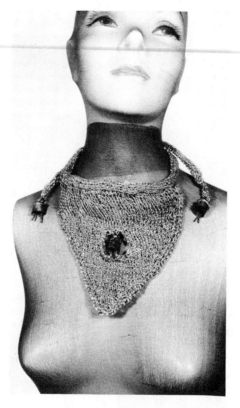

Fig. 4.12 Necklace knit with copper cord, with copper bell accents.

    The illustrated necklace was knitted with copper cord which creates the look of real copper but offers somewhat more pliability. The necklace was started at the neck with a narrow band of one row knit, one row purl. Long bands of knitting tend to form into natural tubes and require no seaming together. A crochet hook was used to pick up stitches from the edge of the neck band and place them, one at a time, onto the knitting needle. This is the easiest way of casting on from one piece of knitting to another. The knitting then proceeded in a triangle shape. The hole for the copper bell was made by knitting to the beginning of the space, binding off five or six stitches and putting the remaining stitches on a stitch holder. The stitches on the needle were knit back and forth until the hole was as big as desired. Then these stitches were put on a holder and the others knit to match in height. When the knitting continued straight across the row, the stitches previously bound off were cast on again.

**_Creative
Knitting_** Ron King learned to knit from his mother as a youngster (his father is a crocheter). As a weaving student at Cranbrook he felt a need to develop a looser technique and so it seemed only natural to reactivate his knitting skills. He has been doing innovative knitting ever since, mostly in jute and sisal.

Fig. 4.13 This woven knit began with a 500-foot length of knitted jute. As mentioned previously, bands of knitting form natural tubes. The knitted bands were dip dyed at five-foot intervals. To fluff up the jute, it was machine washed and dried, then woven. Photographed at the Hadler Galleries.

Fig. 4.14 Side view of Ron King's woven knit hanging.

Fig. 4.15 For the non-knitter, impatient and/or thrifty, consider a pillow woven with strips of knitting recycled from an outmoded sweater.

Fig. 4.16 Ron King's weaving background is again apparent in this handsome natural jute hanging. *Locoown* is from the collection of Robert Pfannebecker. Photo courtesy of the artist.

72

Fig. 4.17 Knitted strips are appliqued to an eight-foot by four-foot knitted fabric of wool and linen. Ron King.

TUBULAR KNITTING

Tubular shapes can be knitted in several ways: (1) The knitting can be divided onto three or more needles, with an extra needle used to knit. As the stitches on each needle are knitted, the needle which held the stitches becomes the "extra." The movement is round and round, not back and forth. (2) Circular knitting needles, available in all yarn stores, can be used for tubular and straight knitting. These are useful only for wide tubes. (3) Narrow tubes can be made on spools such as the knitting toys sold in variety stores or on toy knitting rakes. For greater size variety, rakes can be constructed with wood and simple tools. (4) When working with heavy yarns it is often easiest to knit one or two flat pieces and seam the tube with invisible weaving stitches.

Fig. 4.18 Nancy Cohen used a simple spool to create an elegant tubular knit neckpiece. Her fibers were silver and gold wire.

Fig. 4.19 Norma Minkowitz attached her circular knitting to an antique Singer Sewing machine part. Separate knit bands were added for a fringed surface. Photo of *Knitting Needle Bag*, Kobler-Dyer Studio.

Fig. 4.20 My own cornucopia of sisal was knitted in one piece and shaped with a single seam. The fiber was brush dyed after the knitting was complete. The flowers are discarded colored panty hose stuffed with dyed fleece.

Fig. 4.21 *Angel* was knitted with jute and sisal. Triangular flat knitting was formed into a tube.

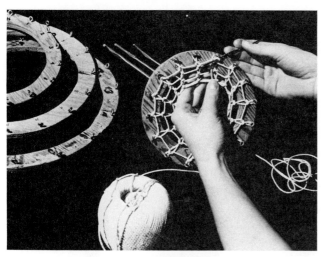

Fig. 4.22 Henry Paque constructed a whole size range of wooden knitting rakes for Joan Michaels Paque. The artist uses a crochet hook to work the loops over the screw eyes. She switches hoop sizes and stitch patterns to achieve variations in pattern and diameter.

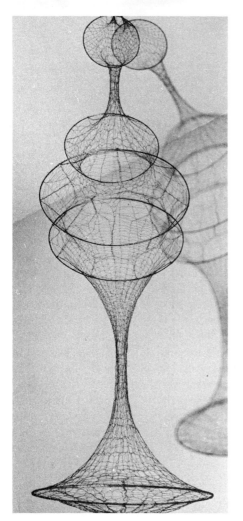

Fig. 4.23 *Space Hangup*, an example of what can emerge from the humble knitting rake. Copper wire is used for the knitting and rings. Joan Michaels Paque. Photo, Henry Paque.

5 Free Form Crochet

Crochet, like knitting, dates back to ancient times. Its history as a fine craft came about somewhat more slowly. For a long time it was considered an adjunct to lace making and was often called nun's work since the ladies of the convent were its chief practitioners. During the Irish Famine, filet crochet, as this type of "lace" was called, was developed as a cottage industry to profitably employ starving Irish men and women. The Irish lace thus produced became very popular and was soon highly regarded by all who bought it. It was some years later, in the United States, that crochet attained a new kind of popularity as a hobby. Once started, crocheters were literally "hooked," though primarily in the production of doilies, table runners and other beautifully executed but rather colorless cottons and wools.

The excitement surrounding fiber crafts in general has of course also translated itself to crochet. Since the early 1960's some of the most fantastic crochet hangings, sculptures and wearable art have emerged from the hooks of artists throughout the world. Crochet has all the advantages of knitting and more, since it can be worked in any direction with just a single tool, the hook. Geometric shapes, ruffles and rounds. . . .anything which one might draw or paint can be crocheted. Stitches can be worked right on to a surface that's crocheted, knitted or woven, making three dimensional surfaces quick and easy to achieve. This easy movement in any which way has made crochet a constant joy and discovery for the contemporary artist.

Crochet hooks are available in a wide range of sizes to accommodate different thicknesses of yarn. For extra heavy fibers, hooks can be carved from dowels, or the fingers can be used. The craft is easy to learn since it consists simply of drawing one loop through another, working in rows or rounds, with one continuous strand. Unlike those working with multi-element fiber crafts, crocheters can add yarn as needed. Since only one loop is on the hook at a time, crochet is even easier to control than knitting. This encourages experimentation since mistakes can be quickly remedied. While there are entire books devoted to crochet stitches, everything is really just a pattern variation of the basic interlooping. The single crochet stitch is the one basic stitch. Familiarity with the taller stitches facilitates shaping, as does the ability to increase and decrease and to go in circles.

LEARNING TO CROCHET

Fig. 5.1 To make a crochet chain, which is the basis for all crochet work, put a slip knot onto the hook.

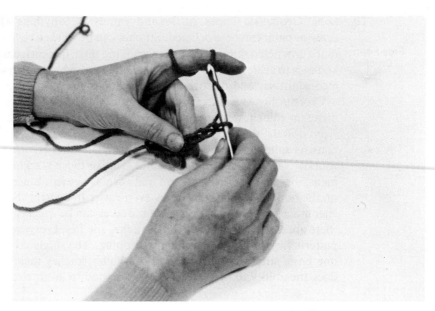

Fig. 5.2 Bring the yarn in front of the hook as shown and pull through the loop on the needle.

Be sure that the hook points in the direction of the chain, since this facilitates pulling the yarn through the loop on the needle in one swoop. Note, too, the way the chain is held between thumb and forefinger of the yarn-holding hand. This helps to create the proper tension and keeps the chain from twisting around.

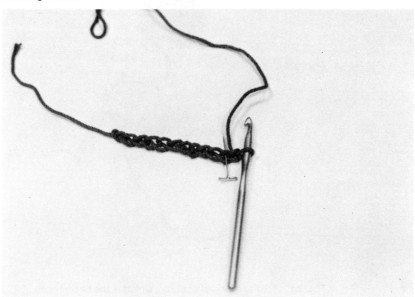

Fig. 5.3 To crochet back along the chain, insert the hook into the chain next to the first one as indicated by the pin in the photo.

Plate 1
Delicate Thoughts
Ceramics, stick weaving, and crochet
(Mary Lou Higgins)

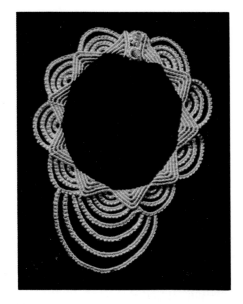

Plate 2
Knotted and tatted necklace
(Joan Michaels Paque)

Plate 4
Chain stitch embroidery on burlap pillow
form (Mary Lou Higgins)

Plate 3
Pot Head. Coiled basket with
separate lid (Madge Copeland)

Plate 17
Fiber sculpture designed for ceiling
of Holiday Inn Airport Lakes
restaurant, 25′ diameter (Libby
Platus)

Plate 18
Nere Eclipse
Partial view of knotted, woven, and
wrapped fiber wall (Leora Stewart)

Plate 1
Delicate Thoughts
Ceramics, stick weaving, and crochet
(Mary Lou Higgins)

Plate 2
Knotted and tatted necklace
(Joan Michaels Paque)

Plate 4
Chain stitch embroidery on burlap pillow
form (Mary Lou Higgins)

Plate 3
Pot Head. Coiled basket with
separate lid (Madge Copeland)

Plate 5
Environment upholstery of French knots on burlap
(Mary Lou Higgins)

Plate 6
Jute dyed with procyon dyes
(Bette Jo Linderman)

Plate 7
Kinetic fiber sculpture in progress
(Bette Jo Linderman)

Plate 8
Dyed, knitted sisal cornucopia with
flowers of colored pantyhose
stuffed with dyed, raw fleece
(author)

Plate 9
Which Came First?
Fiber and ceramic 13″ wide, 36″ high, 21″
deep (Ellen Phillips)

Plate 10
Red Flower Vines (Detail)
Knotting on wire fencing, 3′ by 14′
(Mary Ann Gilles)

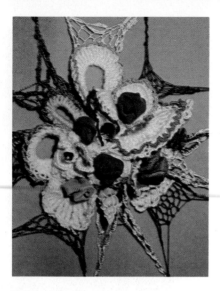

Plate 11
Detached stitchery (Nancy Lipe)

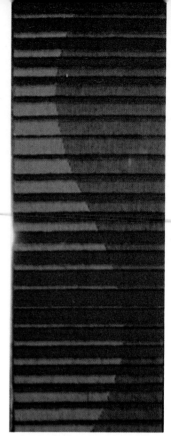

Plate 13
Pin warp vest
(Yvonne Porcella)

Plate 12
Flame stitch "painting" (Joan
Michaels Paque)

Plate 14
Peru
11″ frame loom weaving
(Diane Itter)

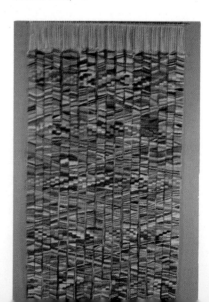

Plate 15
Textured Layered Grid II
Handmade felt and paper combined with industrial felt and metal fixtures
(Debra Rapoport)

Plate 16
Uterine Sea Berceau
Crochet and macrame sculpture, with
lighting (Nancy and Dewey Lipe)

Plate 17
Fiber sculpture designed for ceiling
of Holiday Inn Airport Lakes
restaurant, 25′ diameter (Libby
Platus)

Plate 18
Nere Eclipse
Partial view of knotted, woven, and
wrapped fiber wall (Leora Stewart)

Plate 19
Bobbin lace stitch sampler
(Kaethe and Jules Kliot)

Plate 20
Grew-some
Crochet, stuffed nylon and wood (Annette
Kearney)

Plate 21
Where Eagles Soar
Manipulated burlap relief (Evelyn Svec Ward)

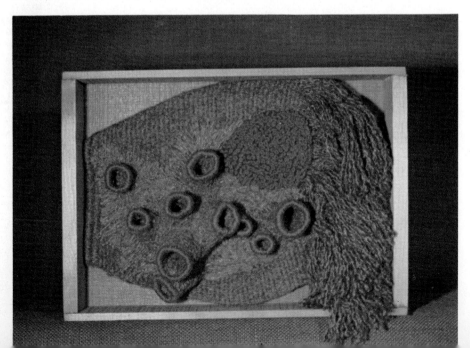

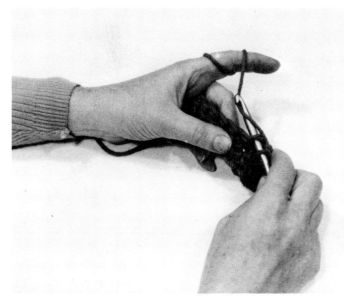

Fig. 5.4 After you've inserted the hook, bring the yarn over as shown and pull through the first loop. Yarn over again and pull through the remaining two loops to complete the single crochet. You always end up with a single loop, no matter what stitch you make.

Fig. 5.5 At the end of the row of single crochets, make two extra chains (this is called *chaining up*) and turn your work around, as shown in the photo. Your turning chain ALWAYS counts as the first stitch of the next row . . . and the hook is always inserted into the chain next to that turning chain.

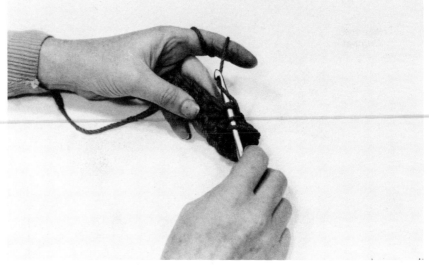

Fig. 5.6 To make a somewhat taller stitch known as a half double crochet, bring the yarn over and then insert the hook into the next chain. Bring the yarn in front of the loops on the hook as shown in the photo, and pull through all three loops at once.

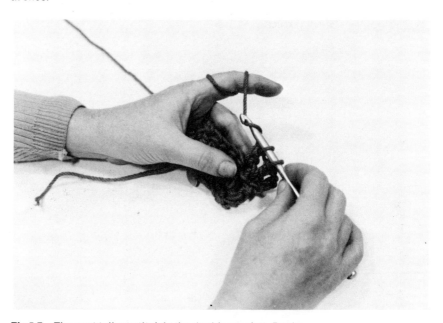

Fig 5.7 The next tallest stitch is the double crochet. Begin this as you would the half double, by bringing the yarn over before inserting the hook into the chain. Instead of pulling the yarn through all three loops, pull it through two only, so that two remain on the hook. Then yarn over again, as shown in the photo, and pull through the remaining two loops. Chain up three stitches, instead of two when you finish the row.

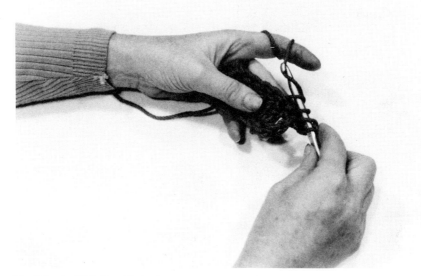

Fig. 5.8 A still taller stitch, the treble crochet, begins by bringing the yarn in front of the hook TWO TIMES. Insert the hook into the next chain and yarn over, as in the photo. Now work off the chains two at a time. In other words, yarn over and pull through two chains three times. Since these are taller stitches, chain up four stitches at the end of the row.

Fig. 5.9 This sample shows the size progression of the stitches just demonstrated.

CROCHETING SHAPES

The ability to create shapes with your hook enables you to really take off. The following information is for some of the most popular and frequently used shapes. There are other ways to work your shapes and still more shapes to make and you'll be able to experiment independently once you understand the concepts which go into these.

Fig 5.10 (a) To make the circle: Make a chain of three stitches. Go twice into each stitch and keep going *around* the base instead of turning to go back in a row. Keep increasing to keep your circle flat. After the first round of increases, taper off the increases by going twice into every other stitch; in the next row go twice into every third stitch, and so forth. (b) To make the half circle at the top right of the photo: Make a chain of six stitches. Turn and do a single crochet into the first chain, two half doubles into the second, three doubles into the middle, and then go back and make two more half doubles and a single. Turn around and work your way back along this curve, without the increases. If you allow the shape to grow, increase every other row to keep the work flat. (c) To make the oval: Make a chain (start with a small oval of seven or nine stitches). Crochet back along the chain. Do not turn around but keep going around the chain. To build the oval, make three stitches at each end of the oval. After the first round make an additional increase by going twice into the stitch before and after the point of the oval. (d) To make the triangle: Start at the point, make a chain of three stitches. Turn and make a stitch directly into the space that is part of the turning chain, and then make another stitch where you normally begin your row (one increase is made). Increase at the beginning of each row to build the triangle. You can start at the wide end, in which case you would crochet two stitches together in order to decrease the shape. By starting at the point of the triangle and reversing yourself at the center, you can make a diamond.

Fig. 5.11 For a circle with an adjustable center, form your yarn into a circle, holding the doubled portion between thumb and forefinger and catching hold of the yarn coming from the ball with your hook.

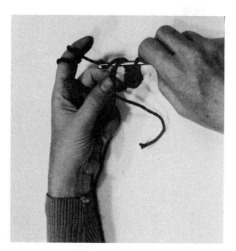

Fig. 5.12 Crochet all around the doubled cord until you have the desired number of stitches for your base. If you want the circle to have a very tight center, grab hold of the short end and pull it tight.

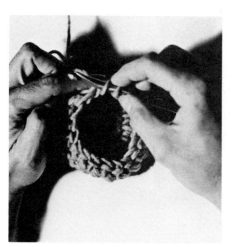

Fig. 5.13 If you want your circles to cup into little tubular shapes which can be stuffed or used to encase hard objects, stop increasing and go around the circle. Now decrease as you go around.

Free-Form
Crochet

The best way to demonstrate the versatility of crocheting different shapes, building one upon the other is to show a large piece as it grew from one central oval shape, with the addition of the other shapes already illustrated. A pallette of greens, golds, oranges and reds predominated.

Swedish Cowhair was the primary yarn used, with some gold rayon cord and a variety of mohairs and velour for the surface texture.

Fig. 5.14   A circle is squared off by crocheting a small triangle at four points.

Fig. 5.15   A small triangle is crocheted along each side of the oval's top point.

Fig. 5.16 When the square is attached to the top of the oval, the triangles from the square and the oval line up. To attach separate crochet pieces like this, place the right sides facing together and slip stitch together. This means that you bring your hook through a chain of each piece, bring the yarn in front and pull through both loops at once.

The plan is for the hanging to grow from the small central oval into a large irregular one. Half circles (see fig. 5.10) are crocheted to the top portions. The bottom is built into a triangular shape by working stitches around the point of the oval. The additions are increased at each side and then decreased back to a point.

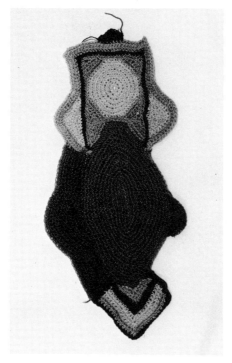

Fig. 5.17 A small triangle is added at the top. This will again be built up with contrasting stripes. More half circles are added to the side of the oval, and spaces between the various protrusions are filled in as seen at the left.

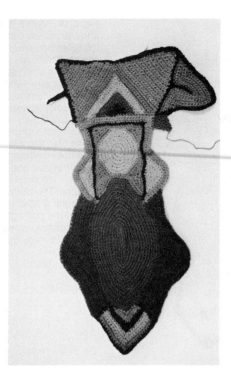

Fig. 5.18   Here we see both sides of the oval filled in, the top triangle built up and again squared off with the addition of larger triangles at either side. At the top left you can see how the scalloped shape on the opposite side was developed: A chain of eight stitches was crocheted at the center of an area. The crocheting goes back and forth and around this protruding chain, with a stitch skipped at either side of the chain's base and three stitches made into the tip.

If you look right underneath the finished scallop shape you will see a little diamond shape. This was made by crocheting from one side of a corner area to another, always skipping a chain before reaching the corner and thus letting the form push out into the diamond shape.

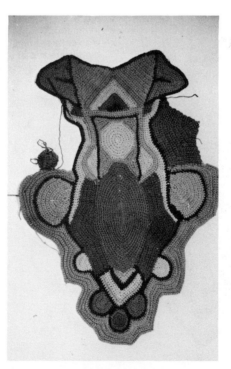

Fig. 5.19   As the piece grows and grows you can see the pattern of adding angular and round shapes.

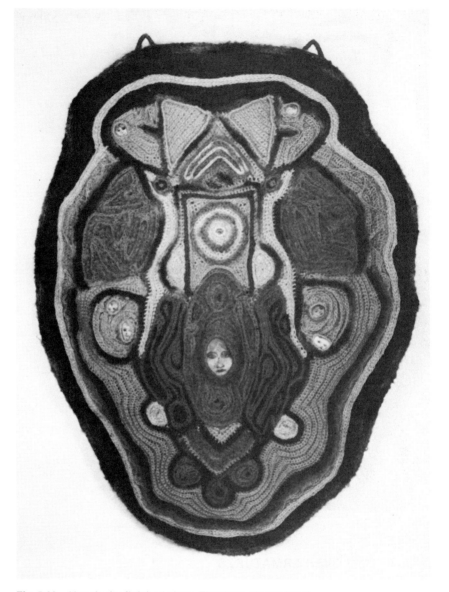

Fig. 5.20   Here is the finished piece. The three-dimensional surface was created by crocheting right on top of the base form with single crochet stitches, worked in a meandering free-form pattern. In contrast to the smooth cowhair of the base shapes, the built-up areas are crocheted with gold cord and mohair and some velour. Some of the round pockets are made like the tubular form illustrated in fig. 3.13. Into some of these pockets, stones with ink-drawn faces were worked, with extra rows of decreases made to hold the stones securely. The finished hanging was stuffed with dacron and stitched to a backing of vinylized burlap. The hanging hooks are made like the wrapped rings illustrated in Chapter 3, figs. 3.7 through 3.10. *Lost in the Forest* is owned by Trudy and Sol Schwartz (see color section).   2½ ' × 3½ '

Fig. 5.21 Detail of *Lost in the Forest*

CROCHETING OVER ARMATURES

Nancy and Dewey Lipe combine their talents to create fiber works which are truly breathtaking. They use mesh and wire rings to support their large forms and are often inspired by their love of the sea. The Lipes let us share the development of one of their latest sculptures, *Uterine Sea Berceau*. The sculpture was made in two halves of shaped chicken wire covered with white sheeting. While Dewey sewed and stitched some of the sheeting in place, Nancy crocheted.

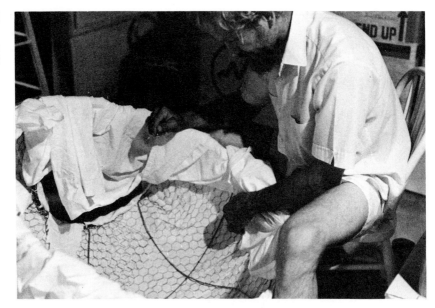

Fig. 5.22 Dewey Lipe sews sheeting around the wire armature.

Fig. 5.23 Nancy Lipe crochets the lining. The base is worked like a large hat in a filet crochet pattern. This means that one crochets a double crochet stitch, followed by a chain stitch to create a space . . . a double crochet, a chain-stitch space, a double crochet, etc. The surface forms are crocheted on top.

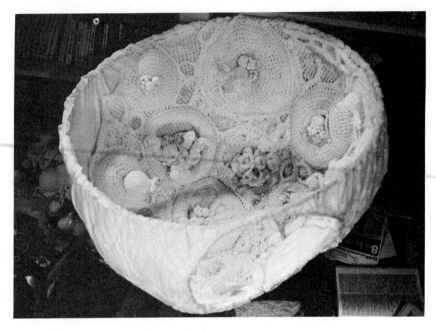

Fig. 5.24 The inside lining is sewn in place.

Fig. 5.25 Large crocheted circles, again on a filet crochet base, are stitched to the outside of the top half of the sculpture.

Fig. 5.26 Wire and cloth spiders are part of the spectacular interior.

Fig. 5.27 *Uterine Sea Berceau,* complete with inner lighting so that its inner mysteries can be fully appreciated (see color section).

Fig. 5.28 In contrast to the Lipe's mammoth sculpture, Walter Notting-ham uses similar crocheting techniques within the parameter of a ten-inch square tapestry. The result is again hauntingly beautiful.

Fig. 5.29 Annette Kearney likes to crochet flowers to go with the natural wood she loves to collect. She stuffs her flowers with natural fleece. The ruffles are made by making lots of stitches into one space.

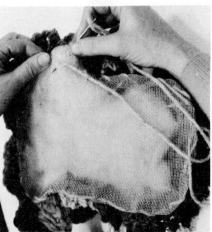

Fig. 5.30 To firm up her forms before stapling them to her wooden base, Annette stuffs the back lightly and stitches on some light wire screening.

Fig. 5.31 Those with a sense of humor can use their hooks most effectively to make amusing statements. For example, Madge Copeland's *Mrs. Jute and Her Jutelings*, photographed by Keith Brewster . . .

Fig. 5.32   or Lynn Myers' wonderful masks.

6 Knotting

Knotting is closely interspersed with the history of lace making. The word *macramé* derives from the Arabic, denoting an ornamental fringe. According to *The Dictionary of Needlework* macramé lace first appeared in the 1493 Sporza Inventory and in a painting of the Supper of Simon of Anaanite now in the Louvre. Knotting was a favorite pastime for sailors, and those who sailed with Columbus are reputed to have bartered articles made by square knotting with the Indians when they first landed upon American soil.

In recent years the astounding number of handbags, belts and plant hangers knotted by hobbyists have threatened to make this new/old pastime a soon-to-pass fad. However, the revived interest in macramé stimulated serious artists who were intrigued with the color and fiber manipulation inherent in the craft. Their work has appeared in many fine galleries and has in turn stirred the consumer to a new acceptance and appreciation of knotted art and has jogged the hobbyist into more imaginative use of materials and designing. Thus, we have today what might almost be termed a second revival, a new nomenclature: Fiber Sculpture.

Macramé is a multi-element textile technique. Numerous strands of fibers are folded in half and looped over a linear or circular foundation, with the ends looped and knotted to form horizontal, vertical or perpendicular designs.

THE BASICS OF MACRAMÉ

The square knot and the double half hitch are the most basic and versatile knots. These can be mastered with little effort and applied to the creation of both two- and three-dimensional pieces.

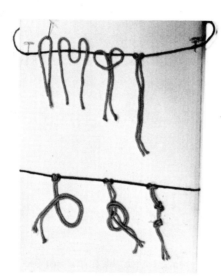

Fig. 6.1 At the top, the steps in mounting cords for macramé. This is called the Lark's Head knot. At bottom, the all-purpose overhand knot.

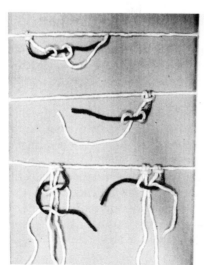

Fig. 6.2 At the top of the photo, the double half hitch is worked from left to right by bringing the second strand of the two Lark's-Headed cords around the first one two times. After a row of left-to-right double half hitches, the procedure can be reversed, as shown in the middle row.

The bottom row shows the two steps for the square knot. At the right we see the first half of the square knot and at left we see how the first step is repeated to complete the square. When the knot is completed, the ends are always pulled tight.

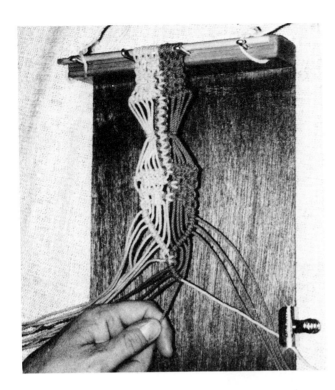

Fig. 6.3 Joan Fetty, who designed this loom to facilitate her knotting, demonstrates how half hitches can be made diagonally, as illustrated, or vertically by changing the direction of the carrier cord around which the knots are tied.

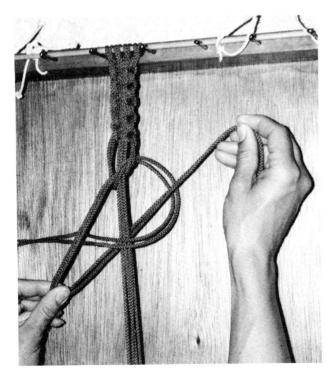

Fig. 6.4 A closeup view of the first half of a square knot being made by Joan Fetty.

Knotting   Since the knot-MAKING cords can be switched at random to become knot-CARRYING cords, the macramé artist has great flexibility in creating color patterns, particularly if the cords are mounted in different colors.

Fig. 6.5   Macramé cords of many colors can be mounted, changing the carriers to knotting cords and back again at random. Diane Itter's *California* is a stunning example of this eccentric weft patterning.

Patterns can also be created by tying a single color as a separate carrier to the top of the holding cord. This separate carrying cord does not have to be pre-measured but can be carried along on a ball, as in knitting or crochet. Only horizontal half hitches are used for Cavandoli work, so named after an Italian lady who used it as a method of teaching macramé to children. If the knotter wants to bring out the pattern, the carrying color cord is used to make the knots, but in a vertical direction. This is exactly like working a cross stitch design, and a graph pattern can be used to map out an exact design, with each square equalling a knot.

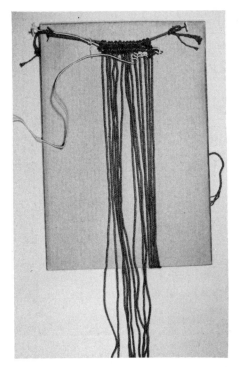

Fig. 6.6 Shiny rayon cord is mounted as a color carrier for Cavandoli work. Since in this case the carrier is a thinner yarn than the mounted cords, the vertical knots are worked three times instead of twice to compensate. The beginner would do best to work with cords of equal weight and texture.

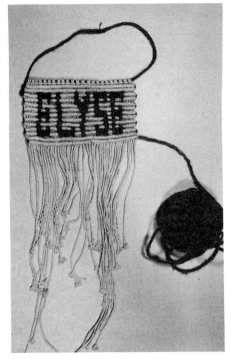

Fig. 6.7 Sol Schwartz designed this very personalized little hanging to illustrate the exactness with which a pattern can be graphed in Cavandoli work.

The next series of photos illustrates the design patterns possible with the two-color Cavandoli methods. These fiber sketches were worked out by Joan Michaels Paque and photographed by Henry Paque.

Fig. 6.8 The design patterns are almost unlimited, as shown by this and the next four figures.

Fig. 6.9

Fig. 6.11

Fig. 6.10

Fig. 6.12

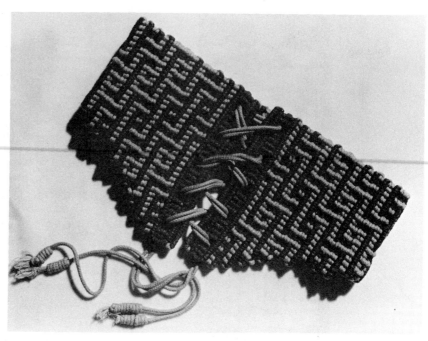

Fig. 6.13 Cavandoli cinch belt.

KNOTTED BODY ORNAMENT FROM A CIRCULAR BASE

In the following series, Victor Comwell photographed Dolly Curtis as she developed a necklace from a circular base. Dolly used jute as a carrying core throughout, as in the Cavandoli method just illustrated. The jute here served as a very solid and continuous carrying core rather than for the purpose of creating any kind of color pattern.

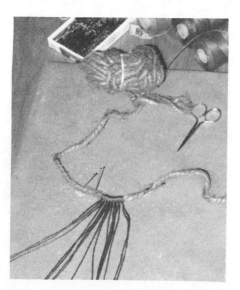

Fig. 6.14 Two-yard lengths of linen thread are mounted right onto the carrying cord with Lark's-Head mountings.

Fig. 6.15 The core is formed into a circle after the first round.

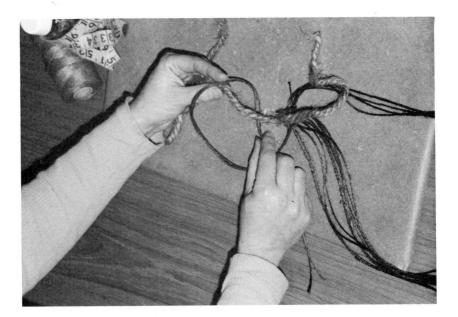

Fig. 6.16 Double half hitches are used throughout. A half hitch is started . . .

Fig. 6.17 . . . and completed.

Fig. 6.18 After the center medallion is complete, the remaining linen threads are divided and twined and wrapped for the back closure.

Fig. 6.19   The necklace complete, with the addition of beads at the front.

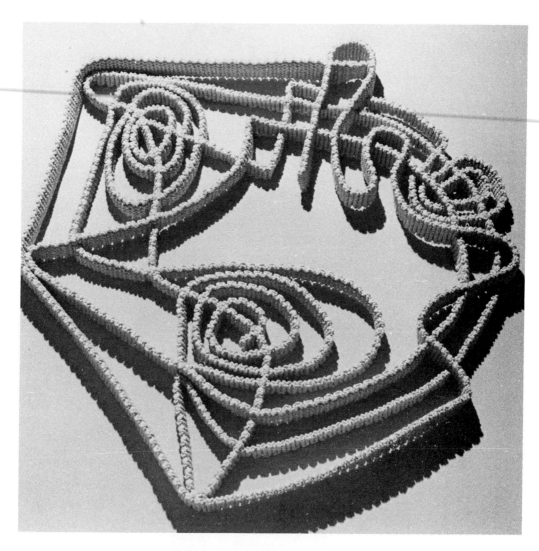

Fig. 6.20 Joan Michaels Paque uses simple horizontal half hitches and strong cotton seine twine to create a self-supporting and integrally connected piece she calls *Penetrating Planes.* Photo Henry Paque.

Fig. 6.21   Detail, *Penetrating Planes.*

Fig. 6.22   *Penetrating Planes* in its early stages.

Fig. 6.23 A trip to Jamaica inspired Mary Anne Gilles to recreate some of the lush foliage. An old fence, once used to corral thirteen puppies, serves as armature and design component for *Red Flower Vines.* 3′ by 14′ (see color section).

Fig. 6.24   Detail, *Red Flower Vines.*

KINETIC FIBER ART

In a paper written for a design seminar class at San Jose State College, Bette Jo Linderman traced the evolution of the woven form, linking each development to a precedent in its sister arts. She concluded with a prediction that since kinetic art was already a factor in other areas, the utilization of elastic fibers in collaboration with a mechanical, kinetic frame could not be far behind. Since then Bette Jo has succeeded in turning her own prediction into reality with a series of three-dimensional macramé and crochet pieces which gently oscillate by virtue of small motors concealed inside the forms. The artist uses wool and jutes subtly dyed with Procyon dyes. These small sculptures beautifully reflect her love of the sea and would be successful even without the innovation of the kinetic concept. Had the motors been less cleverly concealed, the movement not as subtly controlled, the concept might in fact have detracted by appearing TOO much of a novelty.

It's hard to capture completely the sensuous rhythm and almost hypnotic appeal of these fiber sea creatures. However, Robbie Fanning has done her photographic best in her photos of *Polyps* in a sequence of movements shot within about one minute.

Fig. 6.25 *Polyps,* view one.

Fig. 6.26 *Polyps,* view two.

Fig. 6.27 *Polyps,* view three.

7 Knotless Netting and Bobbin Lace

Encyclopedic needlework books have no listing for knotless netting. Illustrations can be found however, by turning to sections on embroidery stitches where it is termed the buttonhole stitch. Sections on Point Laces will see it described in all its variations. . .as point de Brabancon, point de bruxelles, point de grecque, point de Sorrento, and so forth. Modern fiber artists often call it looping, which is exactly what it's all about. Whatever its nomenclature, knotless netting has an enthusiastic following among many fiber artists, especially on the West Coast. Both the open loops of the old-time needlework aficionados and the tight stitches used by Alaskan fishermen for their sturdy containers, are being used to make striking body adornments and large hangings. Knotless netting is often combined with crochet and the two methods have much in common: both can be worked freely, in any direction, flat or three dimensionally. Both offer great flexibility to change color and fibers. Knotless netting is slower than crochet and mistakes are hard to pull out. On the other hand, it's more economical in terms of yarn usage. It is often worked in very small sections and thus easily portable.

KNOTLESS NETTING BASICS

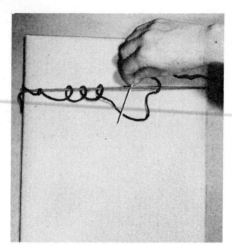

Fig. 7.1 Start looping around a holding cord as shown, or work off the edge of any kind of fabric—crocheted, knitted, or woven.

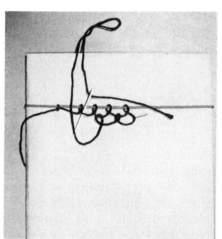

Fig. 7.2 When going back along the first row, pin the loop in place. You could also make a knot to keep the loops from slipping. When working with tight loops, neither pinning nor knotting is necessary.

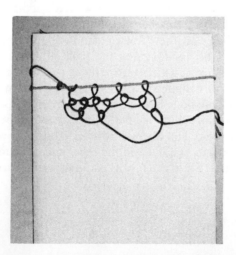

Fig. 7.3 To widen a shape, make several loops into the one above. Loops can be skipped to create negative areas. Shapes can be narrowed by skipping loops. Ruffles can be created by going many times into one of the loops above.

MAKING A KNOTLESS NETTED NECKPIECE WITH CUFFS

Maggie Brosnan combines many small knotless netted forms, some made from linear and some from circular starting cords, to create a striking neckpiece with matching cuffs. The photos of her work are by Lynn Myers.

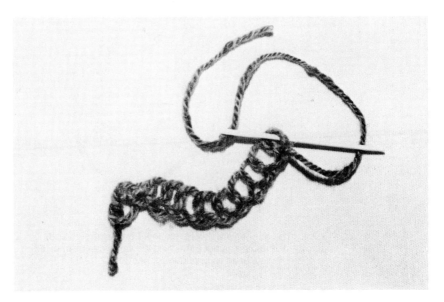

Fig. 7.4 A portion of the necklace started from a linear base.

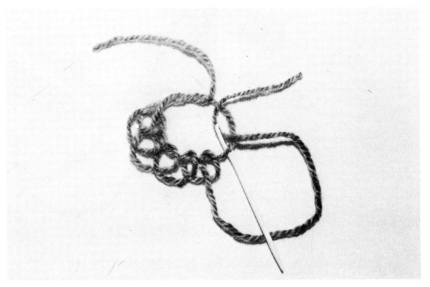

Fig. 7.5 The beginning of a circular form. Note the similarity to starting crochet rounds (see figs. 5.10 and 5.11).

Fig. 7.6 To change yarn, lay in the new fiber as shown and work over it. In looser, lacier patterns, new yarns can be knotted in, with perhaps a bead to hide the connection.

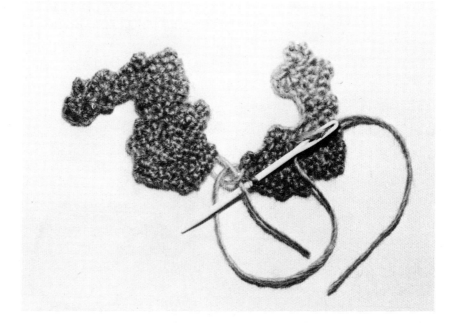

Fig. 7.7 Shapes are looped together to build the overall form.

Fig. 7.8 The finished collar is
accented with a pair of cuffs.

Fig. 7.9 Some wrapping is worked
across the netted surface.

Fig. 7.10 Lynn Myers stitched knotless netting to a leather backing for a handsome bag and . . .

Fig. 7.11 a very wearable jerkin.

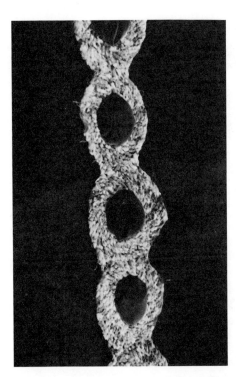

Fig. 7.12 Clydine Peterson borrows from the tradition of the rag rugmaker in this hanging of knotless netted fabric strips, stuffed with velour.

Fig. 7.13 Lori Hansen's *Thought Head Sculpture* combines knotless netting with crochet. The hands are tightly netted with waxed linen. The baby, which is removable, is mostly netted, with random surface crochet areas. The hat is crocheted, with raised crochet worked in circles to achieve the buttonlike look.

Fig. 7.14 A see-through window with wire supports. Aluminum wire was bent into two square frames and each one was covered with yarn. (Wrapping, button hole stitches, or crochet could be used as methods for covering the frame.) The small frame was knotless netted first. Strong blue cord was tied back and forth across the frame, thus providing a random arrangement of holding cords around which to loop a variety of forms. When the inner frame was complete, it was tied to the outer frame, again criss-crossing strong cotton back and forth and using this as a foundation for still more looping. Besides cotton, cowhair, thin weaving yarn, and nylon mohair are used.

KNOTLESS NETTING WITH CROCHET, ON A GRAND SCALE

Libby Platus, who has executed numerous large commissions, started her adventure with fibers at age six, when her grandfather taught her how to sew on a button. "The event is something I will never forget; it was certainly as important and beautiful as a Japanese Tea Ceremony. My grandfather began by introducing me to the thimble. 'We must use a thimble,' he said and I put it on my small finger. It was big and felt stiff and awkward. Then he waxed the thread, rubbing it over a piece of paraffin. 'Now we must sew with the thread.' He began to sew the button on—the thread went in and out of the button. He waxed the thread again. He wrapped the thread round and around between the button and the fabric. He waxed the thread yet another time. He continued to repeat the process several times. I sat there staring in wonder—seeing so much time spent on a tiny little button. Every movement he made was important. He knew what he was doing; to my grandfather there was simply no other way to sew on a button."

The process of designing to the requirements and scope of a public space was one Libby had to learn without the security of an established "one way only" procedure. Yet, the dedication to detail and craftsmanship imparted in that long-ago "ceremony" is evident in the following photos. In-process work photos, Stephanie Lampert; installed sculpture, Richard Hinman.

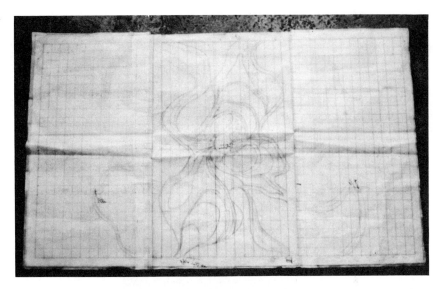

Fig. 7.15 Plans are essential for a large commission. A grid is planned over the drawing of the work so that it can be enlarged into a floor map.

Fig. 7.16 Materials to be used are storaged for easy access.

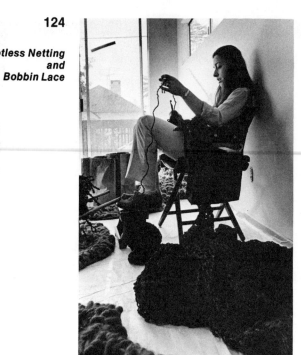

Fig. 7.17 The floor map is tacked in place, and the construction of the fiber strips gets under way.

Fig. 7.18 The fiber strips are piled onto the floor map. Lengths of cable will be cut to secure the work to the ceiling.

Fig. 7.19 An armature to which the strips are attached was lifted to the ceiling with a ratchet puller to do the heavy work.

Fig. 7.20 The artist crochets fiber strips to the cables.

Fig. 7.21 The artist surveys the partially completed work.

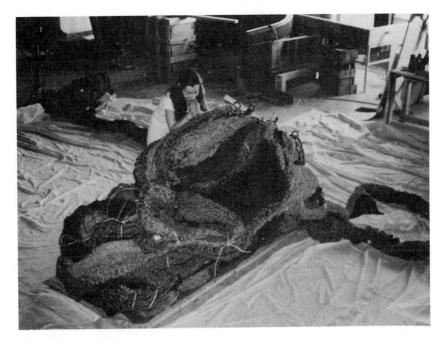

Fig. 7.22   Here it is, ready to be crated and delivered.

Fig. 7.23   The piece is installed on the ceiling of the Airport
Lakes restaurant of the Holiday Inn in Miami.

Fig. 7.24 Another view, showing details of the installation.

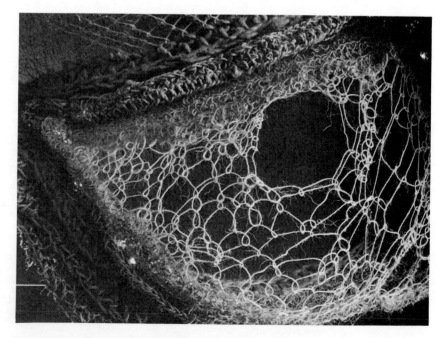

Fig. 7.25 Detail view of the interrelationship between crochet
and knotless netting.

BOBBIN LACE

Bobbin lace is yet another method of inter-looping fibers. Lengths or warps of fiber are twisted and crossed to produce both flat and three-dimensional designs. Traditionally, the lace is worked on a pillow so that pins can be easily inserted to hold the threads in place as the design progresses. The uninitiated are often intimidated when they see the many bobbins which might be dangling from a work in progress. However, while many bobbins might be wound and used for one project, there are never more than four bobbins at work at one time.

BOBBIN LACE BASICS

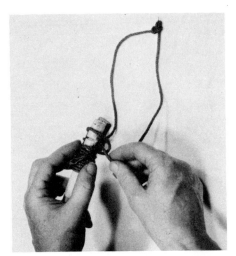

Fig. 7.26 To put your warp onto the bobbin, fold it in half and secure to the board with a pin. Wind the bobbin from the end and secure with a slip knot into the notch near the top of the bobbin. The bobbin used here is an ordinary wood stick with a notch carved about an inch from the top.

Fig. 7.27 The second bobbin is wound so that the two warp yarns are aligned.

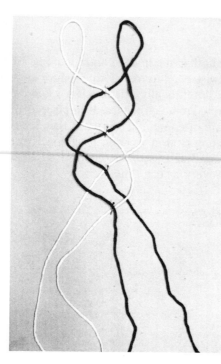

Fig. 7.28 Even though many bobbins may be wound and used for one project, there are never more than four cords interlaced at one time, as seen in this sample of the interlacement pattern. There are two basic hand movements involved. (1) The right bobbin in each hand is passed over the left in each pair, and pulled to produce a twist. (2) The bobbin now on the right is crossed over the left bobbin of the right pair. It's a TWIST first, a CROSSOVER, second.

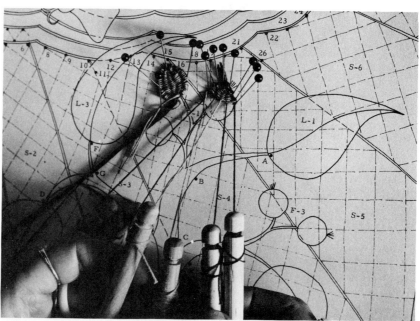

Fig. 7.29 Kaethe Kliot illustrates how a design can be worked by pinning a pattern detailing shape and stitch plan to the pillow surface. The leaf stitch being worked here is one of several bobbin lace stitches.

Fig. 7.30 Kaethe uses different colors to work out the tree branches. Remember, only four bobbins and warp threads are used at one time, so don't let all those bobbins intimidate you.

Fig. 7.31 This small hanging illustrates all the stitch variations possible with this twist and turn method (see color section).

Fig. 7.32 Portions of the design can be used separately as appliques.

Fig. 7.33 Finally, here is a 9½-foot bobbin lace sculpture, again by Kaethe Kliot, exemplifying the limitless art potential of the method. All photos of Kaethe Kliot's work by Jules Kliot.

8 Stitchery: A New Perspective

Stitchery differs from the techniques already discussed in that it utilizes needle and fibers for the surface decoration of fabric and is thus not a method of actual fabric construction. Yet it is an integral link in the long history of textiles and there is ample evidence that stitchery, like all the textile crafts, has been recognized as a basis for innovation. Contemporary stitchers have used their needles to move in new dimensional directions. They have responded imaginatively to new materials, re-interpreted traditional stitches and have combined stitchery with other fiber skills. Stitchery groups are represented in fiber shows everywhere. Classes and workshops abound. The vocabulary of needlepoint and embroidery is so extensive that this chapter cannot begin to give even a rudimentary lesson in techniques, but will instead serve as a springboard for ideas and inspiration.

PAINTING WITH FIBERS

Joan Michaels Paque has executed an entire series of op art fiber paintings, using canvas as her backing and a single up and down stitch. The popular

Florentine work known as bargello is done with straight up and down stitches, but in a zig-zag pattern. The advantage of having a canvas as a background is of course that it is easy to keep one's lines even and plan line width variations for the color pattern. The movement of the needle is similar to horizontal half hitching in macramé, to wrapping, and to soumak weaving. Photos by Henry Paque. (See color section.)

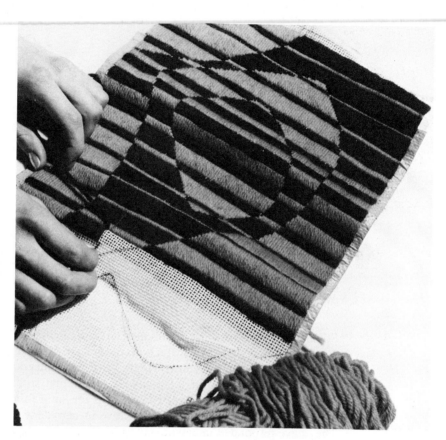

Fig. 8.1 Joan sketches her design outlines directly onto the canvas, using waterproof markers. The basic rows are worked over five holes of the canvas. This base pattern makes it easy to intersperse narrow stripes by making rows covering only two holes or to break up the color within the five-hole pattern to conform to the design plan. Color selection is of great importance to the success of this type of design (see color section).

Fig. 8.2 Op art stitchery painting. Joan Michaels Paque. Photo, Henry Paque.

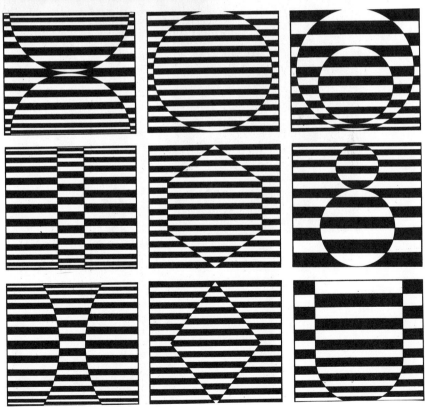

Fig. 8.3 Some op art designs which might be successfully worked in this flame stitch technique.

CHAIN STITCHING WITH NEEDLE OR HOOK

The chain stitch is one of the most popular embroidery stitches. When worked into an open weave fabric with a crochet hook it is called tambour embroidery.

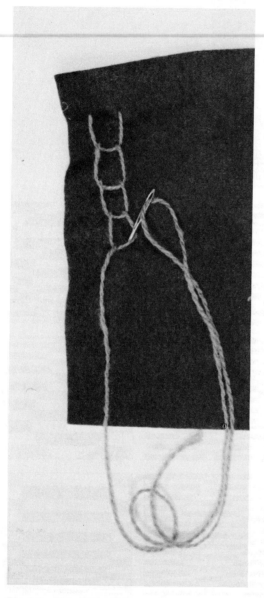

Fig. 8.4 The chain stitch—one of the most popular of all embroidery stitches.

Fig. 8.5 Thick fibers couched underneath chain stitches. *Angel of Death.* Nancy Lipe

Fig. 8.6 Detail view of *Angel of Death.*

Fig. 8.7 Chain stitches made with a crochet hook inserted directly into open-weave fabric such as burlap.

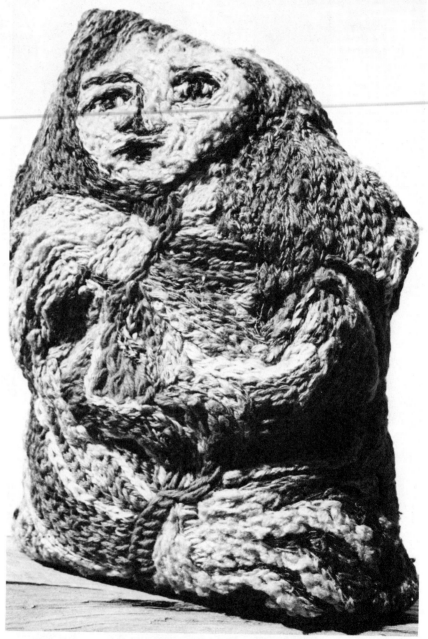

Fig. 8.8 The humble burlap feed bag, stuffed into a huggable pillow form (see color section, Plate 4). Mary Lou Higgins. Photo, Ed Higgins.

THE FABULOUS FRENCH KNOT

French knots are fat, bumpy accent stitches made by wrapping one's needle three times with yarn before inserting into the base fabric. Most embroiderers use them at random rather than in an all-over fashion. While covering a large surface with French knots is indeed time-consuming, it can produce a wonderful surface as illustrated in the following examples by Mary Lou Higgins. Photos, Ed Higgins.

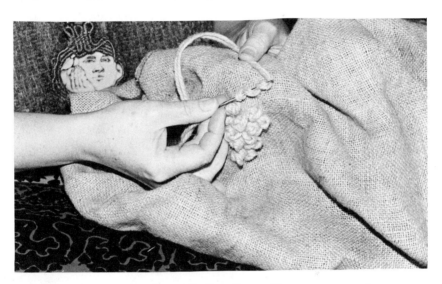

Fig. 8.9 Wrap a blunt tapestry needle three times with doubled yarn . . .

Fig. 8.10 insert the needle into the burlap and out again.

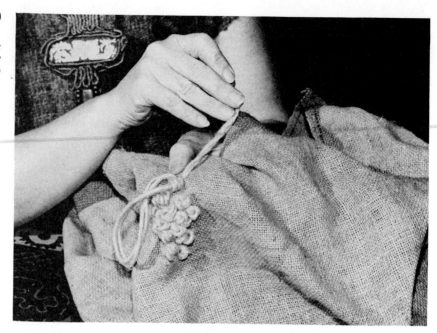

Fig. 8.11 Slowly pull the yarn through.

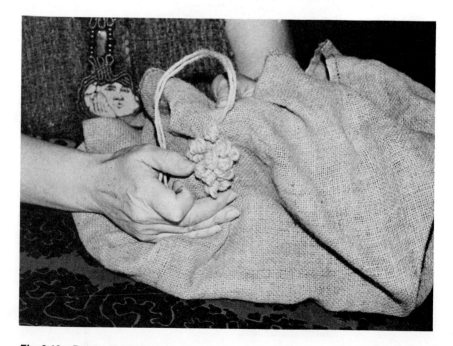

Fig. 8.12 Presto, the French knot.

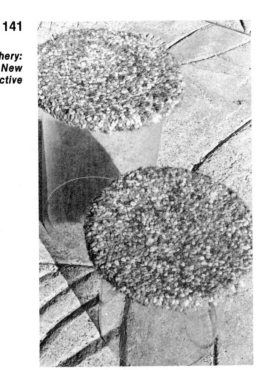

Fig. 8.13 Two stool tops upholstered with French knots.

Fig. 8.14 French knots lend themselves to very simple designs, such as that used for this handsome rug.

(See color section for a whole French knot environment.)

STITCHERY MANIPULATED FABRIC

Its plainness and low cost notwithstanding, burlap seems to arouse a variety of artistic responses. Evelyn Svec Ward manipulates large pieces of burlap into sculptures and reliefs in a way which has imparted to all her work a special and immediately recognizable look. Photos, William E. Ward.

Fig. 8.15 Evelyn Svec Ward at work on one of her manipulated burlap stitcheries.

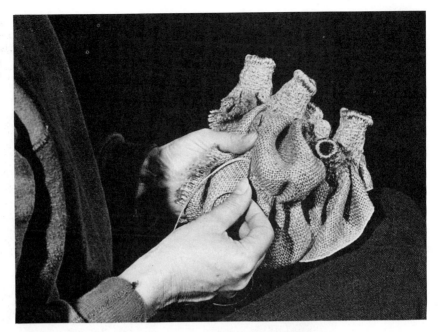

Fig. 8.16 The artist forms a number of different tubes within one piece, starting each tube with rows of running stitches worked in the round.

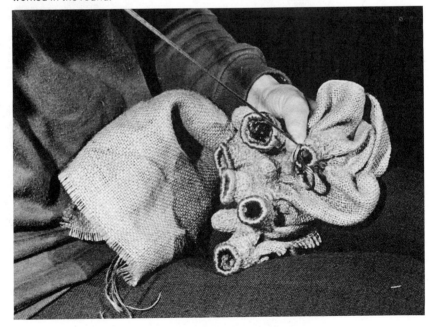

Fig. 8.17 The top of the tubes are either stitched closed or bound with an overcast stitch, again bringing to mind the many similarities from technique to technique, since the movement here is much like wrapping.

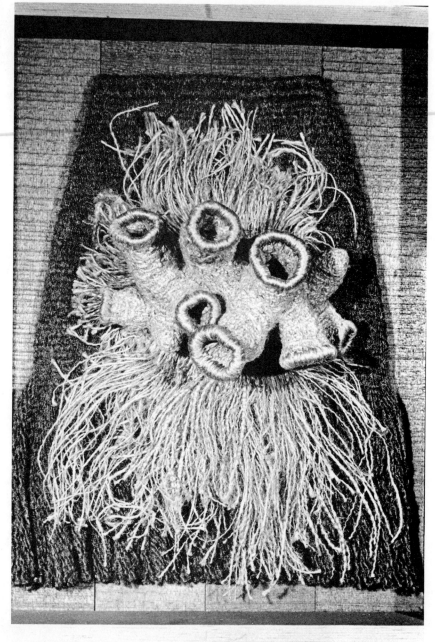

Fig. 8.18 Fiber-manipulated burlap tubes with fringes are appliquéd to wool bought at a Zaootec weaving village. A wooden box frames the relief so aptly titled *Ethereal Dance.*

Fig. 8.19 Needle-manipulated burlap is merged with cotton
threads, sisal rope on linen. *Home of the Cloud Alligator.*
49″ High, 40½ ″ Wide, 7″ Deep.

Fig. 8.20 The stitchery manipulation method literally soars to new conceptual heights in a 76″-tall fiber sculpture. A wooden pole serves as a central support for *Euphoria*.

APPLIQUÉD STITCHERIES

Crocheting, knotless netting and wrapping can be stitched to background materials in what might best be described as detached or appliqué stitchery.

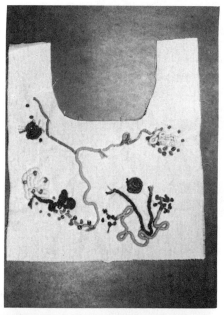

Fig. 8.21 Wrapping and coiling appliquéd to the front of a piece of what will be a vest, once complete. Artist Sally Davidson, adds some French knots to her wrapped and coiled appliqués.

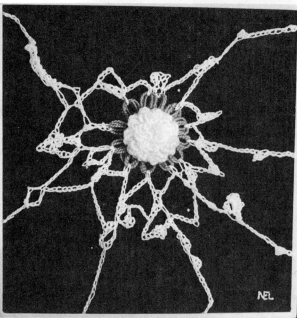

Fig. 8.22 *Loomed Fleur* derives its title from the central shape made on one of those little flower looms available in most notions stores. The embroidery consists of crochet chains. It's all stitched to black velvet. Nancy Lipe.

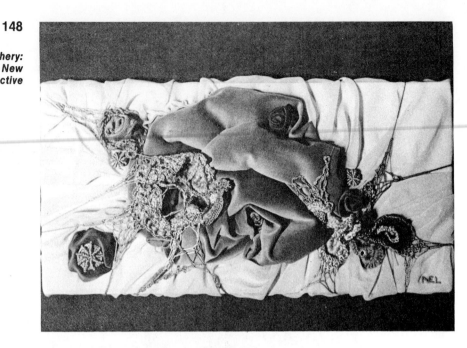

Fig. 8.23 Velvet and chiffon are sensuously draped to
conform to the crocheted and knotless netted embroidery.

Fig. 8.24 Detail view of another of
Nancy Lipe's crocheted and knotless
netted embroideries (see color
section).

Fig. 8.25 Here, Nancy Lipe outlines a brocaded print with crochet chain stitchery to integrate background with the stitchery appliqués.

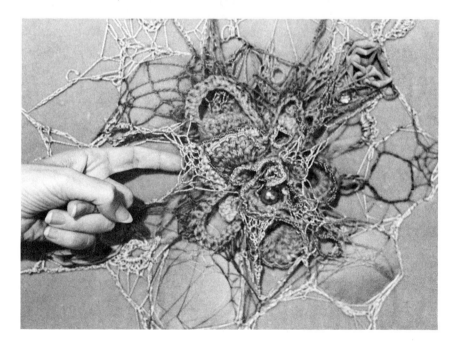

Fig. 8.26 Nancy's stitcheries are tacked down only here and there.

Fig. 8.27 *Sunburst Fleur* is reminiscent of reverse appliqué, since two frames were covered with contrasting fabric. French knots in a variety of fibers, including wool roving, are stitched to the top fabric.

Convergence: A Combination of Methods and Materials

9

Every other year the Handweavers' Guild of America has a national convention which they call Convergence. The convention brings together not just weavers, but all who are interested in related fiber crafts. Workshops in basketry, creative crochet, macramé, and tatting are offered along with those in weaving. Discussions encompass subjects of interest to all fiber people—spinning, dyeing, working on small and large scale, etc. As in this book, everything comes together. Those who weave discover the attractions of crochet; those who knot may try weaving; everybody learns to recognize and appreciate the similarities of some methods, the uniqueness of all. With many ideas from a recent Convergence still bubbling in my mind, I'd like to conclude with this gallery of imaginatively merged methods and materials.

Fig. 9.1 Evelyn Svec Ward successfully marries knitting with a variety of other needlework techniques into a sisal, cotton, and chenille fiber divider. Henry Ward, photo.

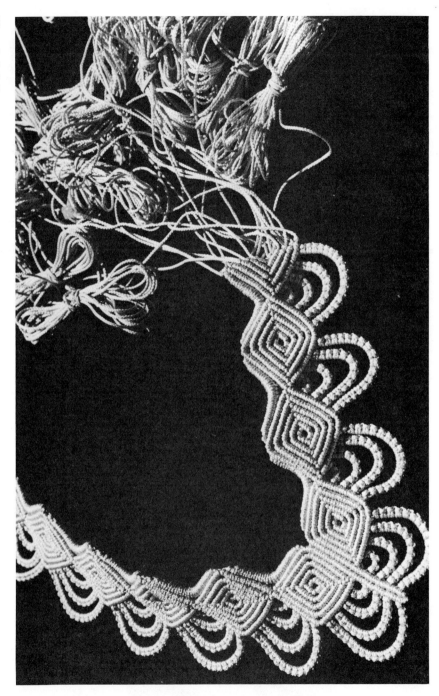

Fig. 9.2 This knotted necklace in progress has a dual crafts
personality by virtue of the loops which are tatted, though
not with traditional tatting bobbins but by finger manipulation.
Joan Michaels Paque. Photo, Henry Paque.

Fig. 9.3 A six-foot by seven-foot frame loom weaving is embellished with little round baskets of crochet, filled with metallic gold yarn. Madge Copeland. Photo, Keith Brewster.

Fig. 9.4 Nancy and Dewey Lipe's ethereal sculpture *Perchance to Dream* called forth their talent for crochet, knotting, knotless netting, and stitchery.

Fig. 9.5 Robert Kirchmyer knots, crochets, and twines wool, cotton cord, and paper into an impressive fiber structure. Photo, Doug Long.

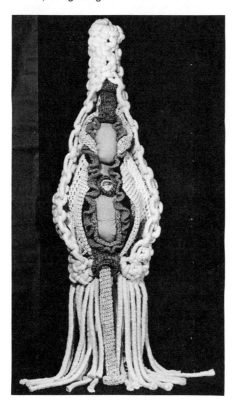

Fig. 9.6 Stuffed fabric adds yet another dimension to a Kirchmyer hanging. Photo, Doug Long.

Fig. 9.7 Many artists seem attracted to the cuddly qualities and inherent humor of stuffed panty hose . . . for example, this fluffy cardboard woven mat, with crocheted food and stuffed hands and arms. Madge Copeland.

Fig. 9.8   Detail view of Madge Copeland's *Meal Men.*

Fig. 9.9   For my own retelling of the Old Woman in the Shoe
story, part of a multi-media series on the population explosion,
stuffed stocking faces seemed just right for the knitted
shoe. A old shoe serves as an armature.

Fig. 9.10 Annette Kearny's stuffed stocking faces are part of a crochet sculpture on wood.

Fig. 9.11 The ceramist can use fibers to echo shapes and colors, as exemplified in this elegant porcelain mirror joined with wrapping and crochet by Kaete Shaw. Photo, Bob Hanson.

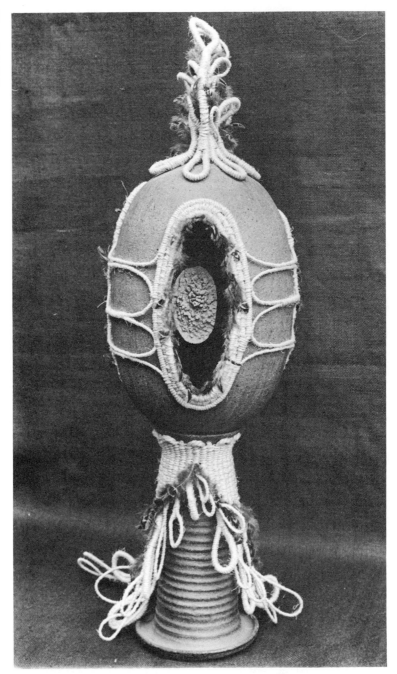

Fig. 9.12 Ellen Phillips identifies herself as a ceramic fiber
artist. *Which Came First* began with the egg and pedestal
with small holes made before firing to accommodate the later
addition of wrapping, twining, and for the interior, stitched
velvet with a natural bone.

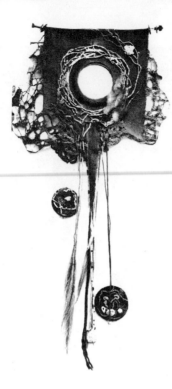

Fig. 9.13 Rae Johnson combines netting and wrapping with leather.

PHOTOGRAPHY, WEAVING, AND CROCHET

For those who bemoan their inability to draw, actual photographs can be used as designs or cartoons for representational weavings. Place one or several photos underneath an opaque project, a fairly inexpensive piece of equipment (around $15). Pin graph paper to the wall, turn the lights off and the projector on. Trace the design projected onto the graph paper. The graphed design can be faithfully followed with the aid of two tape measures placed against the top and side of the loom. The graph paper squares are divided into the tape measured dimensions to determine how much of the warp to weave with a particular weft color. For example, each square might equal ½"or ¼"on the tape measure. I commissioned Mary Lou Higgins to design two portraits, within the confines of approximately eight inches by ten inches. She worked this out in a double weave on a harness loom. However, the method can be applied to any type of loom or weaving pattern. Photos, Ed Higgins.

**Convergence:
A Combination
of Methods
and Materials**

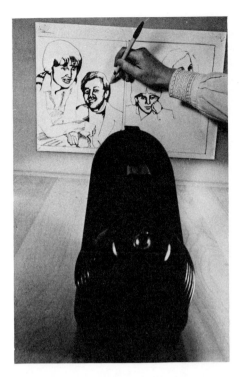

Fig. 9.14 Three different photos are placed underneath the overhead projector and traced onto the graph paper pinned to the wall.

Fig. 9.15 The graphed photo sketch is carefully measured against the warp. This measuring procedure must be followed throughout the weaving. On a frame or cardboard loom it's best to Scotch tape both horizontal and vertical measuring tapes directly to the top and side.

*Convergence:
A Combination
of Methods
and Materials*

Fig. 9.16 The warp ends of the finished weaving are knotted.

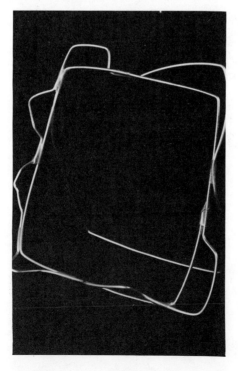

Fig. 9.17 A stand-up frame is fashioned out of aluminum wire.

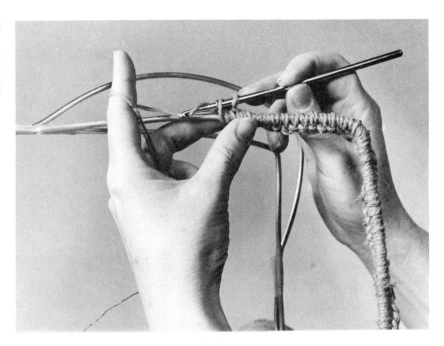

Fig. 9.18 Fiber is crocheted around the frame.

Fig. 9.19 The weaving edges are crocheted and attached to the frame.

Fig. 9.20 The back of the frame is covered.

Fig. 9.21 Brother-Sister portrait.

Fig. 9.22   Husband-Wife Portrait.

THREE FIBER TECHNIQUES FOR ONE FIBER WALL—
MANY HANDS TO CARRY OUT ONE ARTIST'S DESIGN

Whether the reader's involvement with fiber crafts is on a hobby or professional level, this final demonstration of a multi-method tapestry designed for the Knoll Showroom in Dallas, Texas, by New York artist Leora Stewart, and produced with the help of a number of apprentices, should serve to give a better understanding and appreciation of a professional studio operation.

Not everyone is able to work to an exact design or estimate time, labor and materials. Yet, in a commission where the fiber work will function as a permanent wall, it must be pre-planned like any type of architecture. The ability to fit the dimensions of a particular space, and blend the fibers with those surrounding the work is indispensable to the success of the overall.

Nere Eclipse evokes both tranquility and sensual pleasure through a smooth blending of simple methods and muted color, with rich textural effects and flashes of silver. The techniques used are knotting, weaving and wrapping. Fibers used are natural jute, white wool and silver thread. The finished wall measures 10 feet by 14 feet. The photos which follow are by Doug Long

*Convergence:
A Combination
of Methods
and Materials*

Fig. 9.23 Apprentices begin to knot the piece which is suspended from the ceiling. Two separate pieces will be knotted, to be connected by a woven center.

Fig. 9.24 White wool especially plied to the size of the jute is pre-cut and laid into the square knots.

Fig. 9.25 Rear view, showing the connection between weaving and knotting. The warp threads were part of the knotting.

Fig. 9.26 The work progresses. In the forefront are the materials as they were delivered.

Fig. 9.27 An apprentice is seen wrapping, the final phase. Threads were added into the woven section. Wool highlighted with silver threads is used for the wrapping.

Fig. 9.28 Studio shot of the completed piece before shipment to Texas. The entire piece was planned on graph paper to exact scale (see color section).

Bibliography

Abbey, Barbara. *The Complete Book of Knitting*. New York: Viking, A Studio Book, 1971.

Ashley, Clifford W. *The Ashley Book of Knots*. New York: Doubleday & Co., Inc., 1944

Birrell, Vera. *The Textile Arts*. New York: Harper Brothers, 1959.

Caulfield, Sophie Frances Anne, and Seward, Blanche C. *The Dictionary of Needlepoint*. Facsimile editions. New York: Arno Press and Dover Publications, 1972.

Christopher, Frederick John, *Basketry*. New York: Dover Publications, 1952.

Dawson, Mary. *A Complete Guide to Crochet Stitches*. New York: Crown Publishers, 1972.

Dillmont, Therese De. *Encyclopedia of Needlework*. Milhause France, Facsimile edition, Philadelphia, Pa.: Running Press, Inc., 1972.

170

Bibliography

Emery, Irene. *The Primary Structures of Fabric*. Washington, D.C.: The Textile Museum, 1966.

Held, Shirley E. *Weaving, A Handbook for Fiber Craftsmen*. New York: Holt, Rinehart and Winston, 1973.

Lesch, Alma. *Vegetable Dyeing*. New York: Watson-Guptill Publishing Co., 1972.

Macrame, Techniques and Projects, Ed. Sunset Books, Menlo Park, Calif: Lane Publishing Co., 1975.

Mon Tricot Knitting Dictionary. Crown Publishers, 1972.

100 Embroidery Stitches, Coats and Clark Book #150. New York: Coats and Clark, Co., 1973.

Phillips, Mary Walker. *Creative Knitting, A New Art Form*. New York: Van Nostrand Reinyold, 1971.

Schetky, Ethel Jane, and staff, eds. *Dye Plants and Dyeing—A Handbook*. Brooklyn, New York: Brooklyn Botanic Garden, 1964.

Sommer, Elyse and Mike. *A New Look at Crochet*. New York: Crown Publishers, 1975.

Sommer, Elyse, and Mike. *A New Look at Felt: Stitchery, Applique, and Sculpture*. New York: Crown Publishers, 1975.

Sommer, Elyse, and Mike. *Wearable Crafts*. New York: Crown Publishers, 1976.

Thomas, Mary. *Mary Thomas's Embroidery Book*. New York: William Morrow & Co., 1936.

Thomas, Mary. *Mary Thomas's Knitting Book*. New York: Dover Publications, 1972.

Sources of Supplies

Standard yarns are available in most neighborhood stores. A check through your classified directory will help you to turn up greater variety in yarns, as well as accessory items such as beads and feathers. Check under headings such as Weavers' Supplies, Cordage Supplies, Leather, Beads, Feathers and Shells. The following list of mail order suppliers is neither a definitive listing nor one implying any particular personal endorsement. Catalogues are increasingly costly to print and most suppliers charge for sending same. Where no specific charges are listed, be sure to include a self-addressed, stamped envelope (a large manila-sized one is ideal to accommodate odd-sized items).

Broadway Yarns
P.O. Box 1350
Sanford, N.C. 27330
Polyester yarns in heathery colors. $1 for color card, $3 for color card plus one 4-oz. skein

William Condon & Sons
65 Queen St.
Charlottetown, P.E.I., Canada
Yarns

Contessa Yarns
Box 37
Lebanon, Conn. 06247
Novelty yarns

Coulter Studios
118 E. 59th St.
New York, N.Y. 10022
Imported and domestic yarns, weaving equipment, dyes, books

Crafts Kaleidoscope
6551 Ferguson St.
Indianapolis, Ind. 46220
Cords, yarns, beads, books

Dharma Trading Co.
P.O. Box 1288
Berkely, Calif. 94701
Yarns, cords, dyes. Samples, 75¢

Earthguild/Grateful Union
15 Tudor Street
Cambridge, Mass. 02139
A veritable crafts supplies and books supermarket. Catalogue, $2—a book in its own right

Fallbrook House Country Arts
480 Canton Street
Troy, Pa. 96974
Yarns, spinning supplies, feathers, books

Folklorico
Box 625
Palo Alto, Calif.
Their own yarns, plus domestic and imports, dyes, beads, etc., books. Catalogue and samples, 75¢

Goldin, Susan
Box 411
Stony Brook, N.Y. 11790
Spinning supplies

Greentree Ranch Wools
163 N. Carter Lake Rd.
Loveland, Colo. 80537
Imported and domestic yarns, fleeces, dyes, equipment

Lamb's End
165 W. 9 Mile
Ferndale, Mich. 48220
Fibers, feathers, beads, shells, stuffing materials. Samples $1

Lily Mills
Shelby, N.C. 28150
Catalogue, $1

The Mannings
E. Berlin, Pa. 17316
Yarns, cords, equipment, beads, books. Catalogue, $1

Naturalcraft
2199 Bancroft Way
Berkeley, Calif. 94704
Yarns, cords, beads, shells, feathers. Catalogue, $1

Oldebrooke Spinnery
Mountain Road
Lebanon, N.J. 08833
Yarns, weaving and spinning supplies, books

Some Place
2291 Adeline Place
Berkeley, Calif. 94703
Bobbin lace learning equipment plus complete supplies

Straw into Gold
5509 College Avenue
Berkeley, Calif. 94703
Complete fiber supplies. Dye specialists. Catalogue, $1

Yarn Depot, Inc.
545 Sutter St.
San Francisco, Calif. 94102
Yarns, beads, feathers, books